RIBBON

THE ART OF ADORNMENT
RIBBON

NICHOLAS KNIEL AND TIMOTHY WRIGHT
PHOTOGRAPHY BY PARKER CLAYTON SMITH

GIBBS SMITH

TO ENRICH AND INSPIRE HUMANKIND

Salt Lake City | Charleston | Santa Fe | Santa Barbara

First Edition

1 2 3 4 5   08 09 10 11 12

Published by
Gibbs Smith
P.O. Box 667
Layton, Utah 84041

1.800.835.4993 orders
www.gibbs-smith.com

Designed and produced by Debra McQuiston
Art direction and ribbon styling by Nicholas Kniel
Printed and bound in China

Library of Congress Cataloging-in-Publication Data

Kniel, Nicholas.
Ribbon : the art of adornment / Nicholas Kniel and Timothy Wright ;
photographs by Parker Clayton Smith. — 1st ed.
p. cm.
ISBN-13: 978-1-4236-0346-7
ISBN-10: 1-4236-0346-X
1. Ribbon work. 2. Ribbons. I. Wright, Timothy, 1966- II. Title.
TT850.5.K65 2008
677′.76—dc22
2008012992

To anyone who adores ribbon

CONTENTS

FOREWORD

There are few material things in life that I enjoy more than beautiful ribbon. I have been using it for my decorating and artistic endeavors for as long as I can remember. Even as a small child, I would save the tiniest scraps to embellish my treasures. Now, as an adult, I find collecting ribbon hard to resist.

What is it about a spool of ribbon? Holding it in your hand, examining the woven colors, and feeling the textures—there is something special here. Like a tapestry, each yard has its own story, and a fine-quality vintage ribbon can contain so much history within.

Delightful as it is on the spool, with immense potential to become something spectacular, it is also one of the most versatile materials to work with. Whether for entertaining, home décor, fashion embellishment, or a multitude of creative projects, ribbon can be used in so many interesting ways. I use it in almost all of my projects.

My relationship with Nicholas and Timothy started five years ago when I stumbled upon Nicholas Kniel's store in Atlanta. I was amazed that an entire store was devoted to one of my favorite things. In addition to the exquisite selection, Nicholas Kniel offered classes where Timothy taught fascinating ways to use ribbon as embellishment. I was hooked.

Over the years I enjoyed many classes taught by Timothy and countless hours with Nicholas learning about and appreciating ribbon. I have not only broadened my creative repertoire yard by yard, but, in the process, I have built meaningful friendships with both of them.

A wealth of knowledge, passion, and artistry are their gifts, and Nicholas and Timothy are the most qualified people I know to bring the world of ribbon to print and into our homes. A more reliable source of creative inspiration would be difficult to find, and they are constantly reinventing techniques to use ribbon in ways that are beautiful, current, and fashionable.

As I have learned so much from them over the years, I am thrilled they are now able to share their expertise with all of you.

–Kimberly Kennedy

THE RIBBONS
AT NICHOLAS KNIEL

I never consciously set out to open a boutique filled with fine-quality ribbons and embellishments. The number one question I get asked from everyone is: why a ribbon store? Like everything in our lives, one thing simply leads to another. My first job when I was in high school was doing visual displays for a high-end boutique, and throughout high school and college I did visual displays for both small and large companies.

For as long as I can remember, I wanted to be a fashion designer, so I went to college in Atlanta and got my bachelor's degree in fashion design. I designed couture evening and bridal gowns for many years after graduation. I also made many hats and masks over the years for numerous projects and clients. I was thinking I could be the next big fashion house. Unfortunately, Atlanta wasn't quite ready for my couture ideas. I returned to doing visual displays, which led to various interior design projects.

I found that whenever I tried to find great ribbons, flowers, or embellishments for my designs, I inevitably had to call New York or Europe to get what I needed—if I could get it at all. Finding fine-quality ribbons and embellishments was a big problem here in Atlanta, as in much of the country.

My sister was getting married, and I offered to design her wedding gown and trousseau. The gown was a simple yet elegant Edwardian silhouette with minimal ornamentation except for a dozen velvet roses I hand made for the back of the bustle. I found an old book on how to make millinery flowers using fabrics, and that started me on the flower path. The more I thought about it, the more I realized Atlanta needed a resource for fine-quality ribbons and embellishments. At that point I started making plans to open my own boutique and fill it with those high-quality items that I loved: ribbons, buttons, feathers, flowers, masks, and millinery items.

I knew that I wanted to teach skills and pass on some of my knowledge to others. I discussed this with Timothy, who is an excellent artist and poet. We talked continuously about ribbon flowers and how to make them. We found several wonderful old ribbon books, some without instructions, some with. We experimented a bit with the designs we encountered. Some turned out beautifully, others not so! In developing a lot of the flowers, we changed things to make them easier or more realistic as we went along. A lot of what we found in the books were somewhat Victorian looking and simply out of style. I wanted to make flowers that looked *real*.

Timothy and I began teaching our friends how to do the flowers, and everyone always had lots of fun making them. Most found them very easy to make. I couldn't teach classes *and* run my store, so I asked Timothy if he would like to teach ribbon flower classes. He said he would love to try it, and we started developing the classes. We started out with six different ribbon flower classes, and they were a huge hit. Over the years we have had as many as sixteen classes of ribbon flowers and projects. We have created some of our own original flowers and projects and adapted other existing flowers for today. We've certainly lost count of the number of ribbon flowers (thousands, certainly) we have made and sold. After teaching hundreds of students, it's clear everyone loves them. Our students are from all walks of life, from an ex-playboy-bunny waitress to a criminal psychologist. We also have students from all over the country and even internationally, who take classes when they're in town. The interest and the people we've met have been phenomenal. Our friend, CBS Lifestyle contributor Kimberly Kennedy, has taken many of our ribbon flower classes, and *Martha Stewart Weddings* magazine inquired about our ribbon flowers, informing me they were doing a story on the subject. I sent them several ribbon creations for their story, which they graciously accepted for the article.

At the boutique, everyone always asks, how do I use these beautiful ribbons? So over the years I have kept notes on some of my favorite ways to use ribbon. I hope we inspire you to create something beautiful with ribbon and use it on as many things as you can think of. You are only limited by your imagination.

—Nicholas Kniel

RIBBON *and the* ART OF ADORNMENT

RIBBONS ARE AMONG the oldest of adornments in the western world. They are still used today for many of the same purposes for which they were first created, whether practical, such as holding one's hair in place or keeping clothing affixed around the body, or decorative, such as ribbon accents on soft furnishings in the home or on accessories like shoes and handbags.

Ribbon is an elegantly simple idea: a variable length of narrow fabric used for a multitude of purposes. It is wider than string and flatter and more malleable than cord, and it can be woven with any design imaginable in a variety of fibers. Ribbon is also appealing in that one can use it to make a garment or object look sumptuous without great expenditure, an idea that is as relevant to today's consumer as it was to a peasant in seventeenth-century Europe.

ANTIQUITY *and the* CHRISTIAN WORLD

Ribbon adornment was widely used on clothing for both aesthetic and practical purposes in the ancient world, through the Byzantine era, and into Gothic times.

In Egyptian culture, adornment, especially of the head, was favored by both men and women, who wore a type of band on the head called a *fillet*. These narrow bands of metal, leather, or ribbon were wrapped about the head to hold the hair in place. Lengths of ribbon or decorative leather called girdles were used around the waist to smooth out clothing and create attractive folds in linen garments.

In ancient Greece, women wore wide bands of fabric, called *taenia*, in their hair. The winning athletes at the Olympics were awarded red woolen taenia. Ribbons were also used around the waist and upper body to hold in place the often voluminous fabrics worn by the Greeks. The Romans used *clavi*, or colored bands, on their tunics to indicate the wearer's rank. Eventually these were worn by all the classes and evolved into elaborately decorative pieces.

With an immense fondness for jewels, embroidery, and bright colors, Byzantine culture sought to cover everything with ornamentation. Ribbons of fabric embroi-

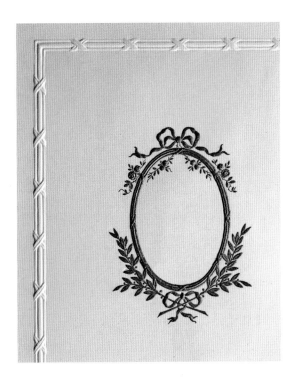

dered with jewels and precious metals edged the popular semicircular cloaks and long tunics of exotic Asian silks worn under coats of elaborate brocades. Richly embroidered ribbon banding could also be found on the superhumeral, or imperial, decorative collar. This adornment, reserved for royalty, was often so heavily embellished with jewels and embroidery that the underlying fabric was obscured. It is the most recognizable element of Byzantine dress.

In the Gothic period, peddlers traveled Europe, selling beautiful ribbons and fabrics from exotic lands. Women tied their snoods—ornamental nets used to hold in the hair—with ribbons. From their waists they hung their distaffs, or spinning tools, on ribbons whose color often indicated marital status. The nobility and the church led the way with elaborate embroidered trimmings of biblical and sometimes figural scenes on garments that set them apart from the rest of society. The Order of the Garter, founded by Edward III around 1348 as a chivalrous fellowship promoting honor, bravery, and knighthood, still uses a dark blue ribbon today as its symbol.

RENAISSANCE SPLENDOR

Ribbons woven with selvedges (finished edges) made their debut during the renaissance, when fashion took on a new importance amid the blossoming of the arts and sciences. For the Italians in particular, clothing reflected the wearer's status. More of the populace could afford fine things, and people actively sought to outdo one another in the elaborateness of their dress. Women began to show their hair more and often wove ribbons into styles set with veils and precious stones. Jewelry was immensely popular, and jeweled pendants were often tied to a lady's sleeve with ribbon. Choice fabrics for the nobility and the successful merchant class included lush brocades and fine velvets, appropriately trimmed with jewels, embroidery, and ribbons, often woven with gold or silver threads. Sleeves heavily adorned with ribbon assumed prominence along with more complex arrangements of fabrics over the newly corseted bodices of women's gowns. Men's doublets grew shorter over hose and were fancifully embellished with fur trim, ribbon edging, and embroidery. Cod pieces became de riguer for fashionable men. These exclusively male accessories could be quite large and fanciful and were often tied with fine ribbons and surmounted by a bow.

ELIZABETHAN *and* RESTORATION ELEGANCE

An array of embellishments such as ribbons, jewels, lace, and embroidery were used in the seventeenth century on a variety of clothing and to ornament soft furnishings. Embellishments appeared everywhere: on gloves, shoes, waists, bonnets, and, of course, in hair.

Ribbons in bows and rosettes graced the wide garters at men's calves, whose elaborate petticoat breeches often sported rows of ribbon loops. These bows grew larger over time, the rosettes more elaborate, sometimes with a jeweled center.

Jewels also competed with ribbons and fine embroidery on the stiff bodices of women wearing large French (wheel-shaped) or Spanish (cone-shaped) farthingales, further adding to the richness of the velvets and brocades used.

Ribbons appeared on the sleeves of both sexes in a variety of styles, and points (metal-tipped ribbons) were used on men's doublets and garters. Ruffled sleeves and the impressive ruff collars unique to the time were tied with ribbons, and the Elizabethan standing collar was sometimes set with small jewels or pearls.

Elizabethans enjoyed May Day celebrations, ancient rituals of Germanic origin, where tall poles festooned with colorful garlands, flags, and streamers of ribbon were danced around to celebrate the arrival of spring.

From 1660 to 1680, ribbons dominated the fashions of the day. Even shoes were adorned with ribbons, the bows often extending past the foot several inches on either side. Ribbons hung from wrists, waists, men's calves, women's shoulders, and elegantly layered sleeves. Ribbon rosettes often encircled men's waists or adorned their cuffed sleeves and large-brimmed furred or plumed hats. France was especially ebullient in its use of ribbon on every conceivable aspect of a garment. Lace was also everywhere, adorning the collars and sleeves of men and women.

ROCOCO, BAROQUE, *and* REVOLUTIONARY TRENDS

The use of ribbon as an adornment in dress and soft furnishings assumed its most extravagant expression in the eighteenth century. Ribbons were often given as gifts for adornment. As always, accessories such as gloves, fans, shoes, and bonnets were embellished with ribbons in many forms.

Paris was the center of European culture, the birthplace of the salon, where eminent personages of the day gathered together in fashionable homes to discuss new ideas. It was the French Court above all others that established the latest fashion trends. Many styles bordered on the decadent as the delicate rococo influence gave way to sumptuous baroque during a time when much of the citizenry of France and Europe struggled with poverty.

The invention of new looms, particularly the Dutch loom, spurred growth in the ribbon industry. Silk manufacture boomed in France, particularly in the ribbon-weaving center of Lyon.

Both men and women adorned themselves with dozens of yards of ribbon trims and flowers. This lavish use of ribbons on clothing among royalty and the aristocracy, along with the elaborate, whimsical head fashions of the time, were epitomized by both Madame de Pompadour and the celebrated, though notorious, French queen Marie Antoinette. Period portraits by such artists as Boucher and Watteau reveal the wealth of ribbon used. Eschelles, or ladders of horizontal ribbon bows, adorned

sumptuous stomachers. Ruched (gathered) and pleated ribbons embellished vast skirts over wire or wicker panniers, or hoops. These trimmings were often moved from one elaborate gown or garment to the next when the original wore out or the wearer desired a new look.

The English city of Coventry was also a center of ribbon manufacture, and the English were equally enamored of ribbon embellishments, as proven by numerous paintings of the time by the luminous portraitist William Gainsborough. In America, however, clothing was more austere as befitted the growing colonies, perhaps a deliberate contrast to the English Court of the time.

During the French Revolution and the terrors of "Madame Guillotine," as the infamous new device was nicknamed, family members of executed victims attended victim's balls. The attendees often wore a thin red ribbon around the neck, and ladies wore their hair "a la victime": piled up and forward on their heads in memory of the executions. The use of black ribbon on garments was stimulated by the vast number of politically expedient deaths at the hands of revolutionary courts.

The cockade, a millinery staple, became one of the symbols of the Revolution. Made from tri-striped red, white, and blue ribbon, cockades where worn on both bicorne hats and on fitted jackets.

DIRECTOIRE *and* EMPIRE

After the Revolution, the French adapted the Directoire style, which turned its eye to the appealing simplicity and the elegantly spare aesthetics of the classical world, particularly Greece and Rome. Fashion followed the new idealism and broke with previous frivolity and transitional styles in favor of short-sleeved long columnar gowns cinched just below the bust, sometimes with ribbon, and edged with less extravagant trims. These were a direct interpretation of the Greek *chiton*, the draped garment most emblematic of the classical world. Women wore their hair up with elegant bands of ribbon, which continued to appear in various forms on gowns, gloves, bonnets, men's bicorne hats, military uniforms, and soft furnishings. Picot-edged ribbon was introduced, becoming all the rage for the fashionable set.

Napoleon's influence was expressed in the grander Empire style. He played an active role in promoting French fashion and forbade women from wearing the same dress to court twice. His empress, Josephine, was the fashion icon of the time. As court styles grew in grandiosity—along with the Emperor's appetite for conquest—so too did the profusion of ribbons and other trims, including fur. Fabrics grew more extravagant; velvet became popular once more along with embroidered silks and the new jacquards. Military tapes, jacquards, and medal ribbons were used to embody the highest honors given by nations.

THE ROMANTIC ERA
and the VICTORIANS

The Romantic era saw ribbon trimmings continue to grow in popularity as bonnets and hats grew more impressive and heavily adorned. Elaborate flowered headdresses festooned with ribbons and feathers appeared on women. The waistline of gowns dropped, skirts became fuller, and sleeves ballooned for a time. Muslin dresses appeared with grosgrain ribbon belts that were delicately embroidered. Ball gowns were lavishly ornamented with ribbon trims, exquisite embroidery, and lace.

Women in Victorian England and the rest of Europe loved to adorn their interiors and their clothing with voluminous ribbons and embroidery. As seen in portraits and the extremely popular fashion journals of the time, huge hats, myriad bonnets, and elaborate gowns with bustles were the order of the day. The reappearance of the corset restricted the physical movements of women, who, though more learned and independent, remained firmly in charge of the home. The needle arts underwent a mini-renaissance, and Europe was in the last big ribbon craze. Hats, cloaks, dresses, and underclothes used yards of ribbon. Soft furnishings in living rooms and boudoirs were dressed with delicate ribbon trims. Crazy quilts of various fine fabrics and lace were embroidered with silk threads and ribbons. Ribbon embroidery became a popular needlecraft. Lovers and secret admirers exchanged ribbon-tied tussie-mussies (nosegays of flowers), in turn decoding the hidden messages in the diminutive bouquets. The development of synthetic fibers and paper for gift wrap allowed gifts to be adorned with fanciful ribbons and bows.

LA BELLE ÉPOQUE *and the* NEW CENTURY

Fashion became less elaborately embellished during the late nineteenth century and the early years of the twentieth century, though it was no less sumptuous, as seen in society portraits of the time, such as those of American John Singer Sargent. Ribbons appeared in women's upswept hairstyles, such as the simple but lovely chignons. They continued to adorn the huge hats of the time that were veritable aviaries of fowl, and were used to gorgeous effect on dresses and evening gowns. Bustles were abandoned, and the elegantly cinched waists of silk day dresses in the wholesome Gibson Girl style, as epitomized in the illustrations of Charles Dana Gibson, were tied with wide silk ribbons that sometimes hung almost down to the hem.

Before and after the two world wars, Paris sought to assert itself as the epicenter of fashion. When it came to embellishment, couture moved in and out of periods of austerity and excess but never to the extent of the previous century. Embroidery and beaded appliqué dominated, though ribbons continued to make an appearance.

The 1920s and 1930s saw handbooks for the domestic arts appear, showing women how to make ribbon flowers and adornments on their own. Women could also order small handbooks out of magazines illustrating the latest ribbon accessories from Paris. These books gave women ideas not only for their hats and clothing but also for items in their boudoirs. Powder puffs, lingerie bags, eye masks, and garters were just some of the items women could buy instructions for and decorate with ribbon work. Wartime shortages ensured that ribbons and other embellishments were reused in new and useful ways.

THE NEW LOOK *and the* REBIRTH OF COUTURE

After World War II, the introduction of French couturier Christian Dior's "New Look" electrified the fashion world. Clothing took on a new, more sophisticated luxuriousness, though ribbon ornaments and flowers were still very much in vogue. Ribbon flowers, large and small, were embroidered on evening gowns, jackets, and purses. Striking looks were created with ribbon and millinery flowers on hats and veils as well.

United States First Lady Jacqueline Bouvier Kennedy brought back the cockade in the 1960s when she had a version of it made to match her day suits. A true fashion icon, she celebrated her French heritage while embodying the best of American style in the postwar era.

In the 1980s, wired ribbon made an appearance and created renewed interest in the floral, home design, and crafts markets. The art of gift giving and presentation assumed a new prominence as well, with ribbons and wrapping paper available in a dizzying array of colors and styles. Ribbon took on a socially prominent role as AIDS awareness ribbons began to appear on lapels, followed by pink breast cancer ribbons and a host of others.

Ribbons continued to be used in the ancient, time-honored role as awards in horse races, state fairs, the military, pageants, and ribbon-cutting ceremonies.

The New Millennium:
Revisiting *the* Past

The move into the new millennium saw the reemergence of ribbon as an embellishment. Couture houses have seemingly discovered the elegance of ribbon all over again. Evening clothes for women frequently echo the past in yards of silks, velvets, and synthetic fibers embellished with lush ribbons, embroidery, sequins, and faux jewels. Ribbon is used in jewelry, tying together strands of pearls or woven into necklaces with jewels. Millinery flowers have moved from hats to the lapel or shoulder, and many of these are made of fine ribbons.

Deconstructed fashions are not immune, as even those deliberately threadbare and worn pieces are laden with crushed, torn, and vintage-style ribbons. The vintage look and vintage clothing is immensely popular. Ribbon embellishments from the past can be seen making a fashionable reappearance on original pieces of clothing or resurrected on new clothing that reinterprets older styles for today.

With home design networks on television and new decorating mavens making the

scene, a renewed interest in home design and décor has led to a resurgence of ribbon embellishment in home furnishings. Needlecrafts, particularly knitting and quilting, have also utilized fine ribbons in various ways. Ribbon embroidery is popular again.

The continued interest in the art of entertaining and gift giving ensures that ribbons continue to grace elegantly laid tables and adorn beautifully wrapped packages.

Ribbon manufacturers continue to create and innovate a vast array of beautiful ribbons for consumers the world over. Today the highest-quality ribbons are manufactured in France, Switzerland, and Japan. The United States also has several fine ribbon manufacturers.

Ribbons throughout time have enhanced the beauty of dress and home and have symbolized many things in many cultures, including triumph, sorrow, hope, wealth, and excess. This ancient form of embellishment continues to enrich our lives and our culture today.

RIBBON AS SYMBOL

RIBBONS NOT ONLY allow us to embellish our clothes and our bodies, they also serve as visual social indicators of personal accolades, shared interests, and support of various social causes. Though we may live in a fast-paced world bombarded by information and technology, the simplicity with which ribbons convey meaning ensures they are very much in use today.

It is common to see various awareness ribbons on the lapels of individuals daily, each person displaying his or her support for a chosen cause. In the service industry, ribbons are often given out to employees to wear as they exceed established levels of standard. It is amazing that a few inches of ribbon have become so ubiquitous for these purposes.

RIBBON *for* AWARDS

Humans have always felt a need to bestow honor on individuals who have proven themselves worthy or performed an extraordinary service. Unlike trophies or certificates, ribbons can be worn on the body as a visual emblem of achievement, allowing the honoree to remind society of his or her accolades outside the confines of awards ceremonies and the home. The prestige afforded by such awards helps to set an example of excellence, and wearing a ribbon or ribbon badge allows one to do this with ease rather than pomposity.

Ribbons have long represented excellence; think of blue ribbons won at county fairs—these ribbons descend from The Order of the Garter. Members of the Order still wear blue sashes as a symbol of their prestige today. Ironically, in our commerce-driven world, the blue ribbon is also used extensively as a sign of quality for product advertising. The Olympic games and other sporting events bestow medals that hang from ribbons. There are thousands of amateur events, such as running, swimming, even shooting, that use ribbons for medals. Many people collect them as a visual record of achievement.

A show horse proudly wears an equestrian ribbon,
which is among the showiest of ribbon awards
with a large rosette and long tails.

NEWTON
COUNTY
SADDLE
CLUB

DIVISION HIGH POINT

CHAMPION

Animal clubs and societies regularly have shows where animals are judged and awarded ribbons. An exceptional horse might win an array of colorful ribbons for his young owner to hang on her wall. A fine pig, sheep, or rooster at the fair might do so as well for the boy who has carefully tended his charge.

The military has many medals and ribbon bars it bestows on servicemen and service-women, such as the Purple Heart for those who are wounded in battle and the Medal of Honor for those who have displayed the utmost bravery. Service bars of ribbon worn on the uniform serve as a visual record of one's service history, achievements, and pro-ficiencies. Military ribbons represent an appreciation for the excellence of service and, in some cases, the sacrifices made by existing service members and veterans.

YELLOW RIBBONS

Like the blue ribbon, the yellow ribbon has attained a cultural status above ribbons of other colors, along with the red AIDS and pink breast cancer ribbons of recent decades. It could truly be called the original awareness ribbon, used to remember loved ones away at war and to symbolize hope for their safe return. We all know the songs "She Wore a Yellow Ribbon" and "Tie a Yellow Ribbon 'Round the Old Oak Tree." In recent years this bittersweet symbol has seen a resurrection on lapels, cars, and, yes, tree trunks.

An impressively detailed vintage military medal
hangs from a fine-striped grosgrain.

RIBBON *and* SOCIAL AWARENESS

It started with the red ribbon. Formed into a simple loop and worn on a lapel, the AIDS awareness ribbon arose out of a desperate need to bring attention to the devastation wrought by a new, frightening disease that suddenly appeared in the early 1980s. The ribbon was conceived of by an organization called Visual AIDS, which enlisted artists to create a symbol that could be used as a visual means of support and awareness. Ribbons have always lent themselves to the use of the symbolic (such as the yellow ribbon), but this reinvention was a powerful idea due to its sheer simplicity. It made a bold and important statement at a time when the stigma of the disease was strong and when clear scientific information lacking or obscured by lingering hysteria and prejudice. It debuted at the Tony Awards in 1991, worn by British actor Jeremy Irons. It caused a sensation with the media and people everywhere who knew the devastation AIDS could wreak. Soon red ribbons began to appear en masse on lapels around the world, paving the way for new dialogue, support, and awareness. Thus, the awareness ribbon was born.

On the heels of the successful AIDS ribbon, other awareness ribbons began to appear, most notably the pink breast cancer ribbon, perhaps the second most recognized awareness ribbon in the world. This new mode of spreading social awareness was the perfect way to express support for a cause, and so today there are a large number of ribbons of specific colors that are used to promote awareness of various social issues. Colors overlap issues: many organizations share the same colors to promote their individual focus. Though this list is far from exhaustive, the photograph shows a selection of various ribbons, with their causes explained on page 24.

These awareness ribbons use color to symbolize their specific cause, thus helping to make the public more aware of the important issues of today.

White ribbon: Innocence, victims of terrorism, peace, bone cancer, scoliosis, and adoption.

Ivory ribbon: Paralysis, spinal cord injury, and diseases and disorders of the spine.

Gold ribbon: Childhood cancer.

Peach ribbon: Uterine cancer or endometrial cancer.

Orange ribbon: Leukemia, hunger, cultural diversity, and motorcycle safety.

Pale pink ribbon: Breast cancer, birth parents, and cleft palate syndrome.

Dark pink ribbon: Inflammatory breast cancer.

Red ribbon: HIV/AIDS, heart disease, stroke, and substance abuse.

Burgundy ribbon: Brain aneurysm, caesarian section (worn upside down), hospice care, and multiple myeloma.

Lavender ribbon: General cancer awareness, epilepsy, and Rett Syndrome; also a symbol of foster care or foster parents.

Periwinkle ribbon: Eating disorders, esophageal cancer, and pulmonary hypertension.

Purple ribbon: Pancreatic cancer, attention deficit disorder, Alzheimer's disease, religious tolerance, animal abuse, and victims of 9/11.

Yellow ribbon: Support for troops in general and those who are POW/MIA, suicide prevention, missing children, and bladder cancer.

Pale yellow ribbon: Spina bifida awareness.

Pale blue ribbon: Prostate cancer, men's health, thyroid disease, scleroderma, Grave's disease, and childhood cancer.

Turquoise ribbon: Native Americans and Native American reparation.

Teal ribbon: Ovarian and cervical (also uterine) cancers, sexual abuse/assault, tsunami victims, and food allergies.

Dark blue ribbon: Arthritis, child abuse prevention, victim's rights, free speech, and water quality and safety.

Lime green ribbon: Lymphoma, Lyme disease, Ivemark syndrome, and Sandhoff disease.

Green ribbon: Childhood depression, mental health or illness, glaucoma, environmental concerns, tissue donation, and organ transplants.

Brown ribbon: Anti-tobacco and colorectal cancer.

Silver ribbon: Parkinson's disease, children with disabilities, anxiety disorders, bipolar disorder, and severe depression.

Grey ribbon: Diabetes, asthma, and allergies.

Black ribbon: Mourning, melanoma, gang prevention, and also MIAs.

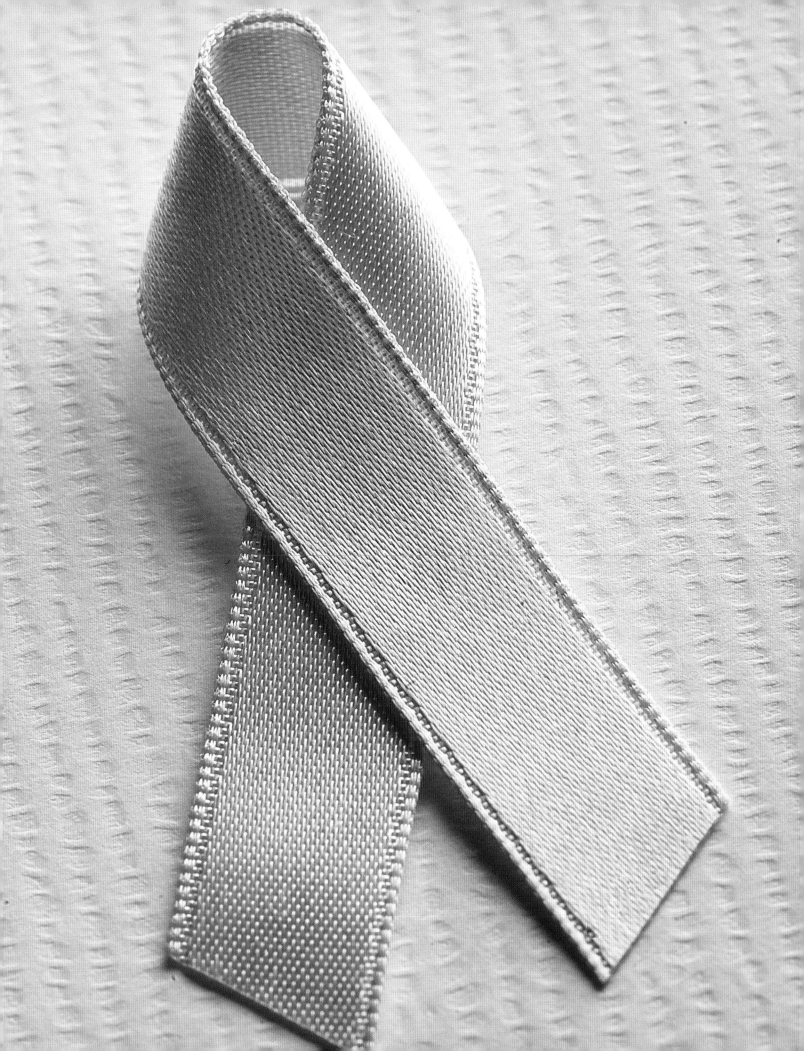

RIBBON IN FASHION

THE QUINTESSENTIAL use for ribbons is on our clothing or bodies. Practical purposes aside, humans feel an almost instinctual need to adorn themselves with items that are pleasing to the eye. Clothing defines our status and what we are about, what social groups we belong to, how we make our living, what ceremonies we are enacting, and even what type of mood we're in. We use clothing to draw others to us in intimate settings or to stand out in a crowd.

In the wide variety of fashions available today, ribbon embellishment is popular among designers and buyers, while the great couture houses have seemingly reinvented the use of ribbon trims overnight on impressive gowns. Ribbon also adorns the everyday article of clothing, from T-shirts and jeans to casual jackets and blouses. Many articles of clothing without embellishment can be made lovelier with ribbons and ribbon trims. Ribbon can also be used extensively for accessories and jewelry.

A found treasure: this vintage photo postcard circa 1913 shows a young girl named Emily proudly wearing a large ribbon in her hair, *facing*. Victorian gowns were often adorned with voluminous amounts of ribbon; in this photograph, a lady of the time wears a gown embellished with a crisp striped ribbon that draws attention to her slender neck, *above left*. This Victorian lady's day dress is accented with numerous ribbon bows down the front of the bodice, *above right*. Little boys did not always escape the use of ribbon as an embellishment. This charming young subject's large bow gives him a bohemian air, *right*.

TIMELESS HAIR

For the all-important look of one's hair, tying it up with ribbons in ponytails, pig-tails, or braids, or placing a classic band over the head and tying it at the nape of the neck can be a refreshing alternative to one's usual style. Ribbon hair bands can be plain or embellished with beads and crystals to give them more "presence." Re-member Dorothy from the Wizard of Oz or the Gibson girl with her massive chignon and ribbon bow? Bows in hair don't have to be girlish, however charming they may be. Sophisticates have been known to pull all of their hair back and hide the bun in a cluster of ribbon bows and to add a feather or two for dramatic effect.

Not just for storybook girls,
ribbon headbands are timeless as
well as stylishly simple.

Rich red satin ribbon elevates *classic pigtails* from girlish to chic, *facing*.

The ponytail as fashion statement originated as a men's hairstyle in the eighteenth century based on horses' tails, *above*.

THE ULTIMATE HAT

Naturally, hats are the place where ribbon is used most frequently for bands, trims, and flowers in conjunction with a host of other millinery trims. Hats are more than utilitarian—they are one of the ultimate fashion accessories with a long pedigree. From eighteenth-century portrait hats to Victorian millinery confections, from turn-of-the-century extravaganzas of fowl, feather, and flowers to diminutive pillboxes of the 1950s, hats have made their mark. Men are well-represented here as well with the elegant top hats and dashing derbies of yesterday (and still today), along with fedoras, classic cowboy hats, and Panama hats, all sporting ribbon bands, various feathers, and other small embellishments. Who can forget Fred Astaire in *Top Hat* or Audrey Hepburn at the derby in *My Fair Lady* with her grand hat and its huge black-and-white striped bow? The black hat she wore in *Breakfast at Tiffany's*, with its long elegant ribbon, perfectly expresses the modern idea of femininity. Hats can be transformed by various choices of ribbon around the crown for bands, clusters of ribbon flowers and cockades mingled with millinery fruits and leaves, or with delicate ribbons woven in seductive veiling. A straw hat with a simple wide band of taffeta and a single millinery flower is all one needs for a day out at the races, the beach, a picnic, or a stroll while window-shopping. Even knitted hats for fall and winter are charming with the addition of a taffeta jeweled rosette or a simple silk satin bow.

Vintage men's hats sporting dapper ribbon bands. In recent years these types of hats, once wardrobe essentials of older gentlemen, have seen a resurgence of popularity among younger men.

his spectacular hat, with its wreath of black taffeta ribbon, elaborate millinery feathers, and dotted veiling, is a derby-goer's dream, *facing*. Yards of ruched velvet ribbon compose much of the embellishment of this richly colored couture hat, *above left*. This fine straw hat is graced with a cluster of millinery berries and a beautiful taffeta ribbon in colors that herald the new season, *above right*. The widest brim, the lushest flowers, and the crispest striped taffeta ribbon combine to make this hat a work of grandeur, *right*.

HANDBAGS *and* PURSES

Ribbon trims, especially bows and flowers in a variety of colors and types, are perfect for handbags. Small, elegant clutches in satin with a cockade or silk satin tuxedo bow are excellent for evening glamour, and the classic tote in straw or canvas with a grosgrain in stripes or polka dots and bright taffeta ribbon roses is perfect for summer outings. Straps on handbags can be replaced with ribbon as well; take care to choose a sturdier grosgrain ribbon for heavier casual bags and a satin for lighter evening bags. Ribbon trims on bags can be attached by stitching, gluing, or using a shoe clip with the trim attached, if you like.

A lady and her handbag.
This elegant little bag is graced with hand-dyed
silk ribbon and a vintage pin—perfect for a
luncheon or evening out.

A vintage clutch turns into a *shoulder bag* with the addition of a satin strap. A vintage button and soft silk ribbon add to the transformation, *facing*. This summer tote is further brightened by the richly colored ribbon rosette and the crisp striped taffeta, *above*.

Securely tie bright ribbons to *personalize your* luggage, making it easier
to keep track of and find at baggage claim when you travel.

FUN *and* SEXY SHOES

Shoes are often forgotten when thinking about embellishment, but they are perfect canvases for ribbons. Ribbons can dress them up, make them flirty, or add an extra touch of elegance. Strappy sandals with ribbon laces look sexy and summery, especially if the ribbon is light and airy, like a bias-cut silk. Shoe clips with bows and cockades are sophisticated and fun, and because clips aren't a permanent embellishment, expensive pairs can be given different looks as well. Tuxedo bows attached to the heels of a pair of high pumps is ever so sexy, drawing the eye to the feet and back of the calves. Buckles can be dressed up with grosgrain for a classic Wasp effect. Adding cockades and flowers of ribbon to boots or simply wrapping ribbons Roman style around the calf is a refreshing way to change up their more substantial presence.

Evening glamour: a pair of high heels encrusted with jewels and frayed silk ribbon catches the eye with sparkle and movement.

Tiny cockade shoe clips *dress up* this plain pair of fuchsia pumps.

*R*ibbon rosettes with jeweled centers and dangling straps of ribbon give a playful military air to the look of this pair of sleek suede boots, *facing and above left.* Slinky heels are dressed with striped satin ribbon and a black patent leather gardenia for a night on the town, *above right and right.*

One of life's ultimate luxuries: a serious pair of gorgeous pumps.
Rhinestone buckles add to the luxuriousness.

the
SHOE CLIP

Shoe clips are easy to customize with a ribbon bow,

cockade, or flower. For example, make two tuxedo bows (stitch them together to hold) out

of 1-inch satin ribbon, choosing a color that accents

your outfit or the shoe itself. Stitch or glue each bow securely to a shoe clip and attach the

clips to a pair of plain shoes (such as satin pumps) for a flirty evening

out. For extra glamour, glue a few diminutive crystals to the knot of the bow.

BELTS *and* SASHES

Belts can be customized out of various ribbons for specific looks and articles of clothing. They can be made of grosgrain for everyday items, like jeans or khakis, or satin for more delicate articles of clothing such as a bias-cut silk skirt. For a simple belt, just cut the ribbon to the right length, finish the ends, and use a d-ring to buckle. In place of a d-ring, you can tie or tuck one end under the other. If you have an individual buckle with jewels or perhaps a vintage one out of mother-of-pearl or silver, a length of ribbon simply threaded through shows it off to great effect.

Dresses, gowns, and blouses are ultrafeminine when a sash is worn, either luxuriously wide or delicate and narrow in ribbons of silk satin or velvet. For example, a little black cocktail dress of black silk satin with an empire waist could dazzle with the addition of a fuchsia-colored satin ribbon across the empire seam and tied in a flirty bow in the back, with tails falling to just above the hem. Try experimenting with ribbons of various colors and textures for sashes. In addition, embellishing ribbon sashes with crystals or sequins turns the luxurious to sumptuous.

New and vintage rhinestone buckles
of various sizes and styles create an elegant belt
for a cocktail or evening dress.

Use vintage mother-of-pearl buckles for a belt, choker, or bracelet, *facing*. This vintage ribbon label tape paired with a rhinestone brooch makes a playful and chic belt or an unconventional sash for a pretty dress, *above left*. Printed ribbon works to add a Parisian flair to jeans with the names of streets in the French capital, *above right*. Double wrapped striped picot grosgrain with love knots and a brooch embellish this pair of jeans, *right*.

DELICIOUS JEWELRY

Ribbon can be worn as or with jewelry in many ways. A simple band of velvet or satin around the neck adorned with a jewel or items such as cameos, pearl drops, or brooches is beautiful and very feminine. Simple bands of velvet can also be embellished with beads and crystals. Longer lengths of ribbon worn with pendants of natural stones and precious metals are always striking. Try tying up a strand (or several) of pearls with a delicious silk satin or bias-cut silk ribbon and wear it with an open-backed garment. On the wrist, a wide band of ribbon with a fabulous brooch evokes the grandeur of the Belle Époque. Rather than using wire or other stringing materials for beads, try using ribbon instead, knotting it on either side of each bead and allowing various bits of its length to show (make sure the ribbon fits through the holes properly).

This beautiful turquoise pendant paired with a lush velvet ribbon brings to mind Elizabethan jewels.

A trio of chunky bangles is given extra flair when accented with ribbon, *facing*. A brooch need not be worn solely on the lapel. Here, a stylized jeweled feather is worn as a choker on a luxuriously wide velvet ribbon, *above left*. Deliberately frayed silk ribbon is used to add soft texture to this lovely set of sizeable beads, *above right*. These gorgeous and chunky stones are less imposing when threaded with a tiny picot ribbon, *right*.

RIBBON PET COLLARS

Ideas for ribbon embellishment on clothing and accessories are only limited by taste and imagination. They are certainly not limited by species: one of our favorite uses of ribbon is for dog collars and leashes. Our good-natured canine companions generally put up with what we humans ask of them (think bandanas, sweaters, coats, and doggie shoes), and if Fido is willing, have him or her sit for a portrait with a gorgeous ribbon bow or jewel-studded satin ribbon collar. Take care not to leave long tails if dogs might walk around when wearing them. For more practical purposes, a leash can be adorned with ribbon either glued or stitched along its length or dangling as a jaunty bow where the leash attaches to the collar. Felines can sometimes be cajoled into wearing a bow for a short period of time, but a ribbon collar makes them regal. Ponies and horses often sport gloriously braided manes with colorful ribbons when in parades or show events.

portrait of an elegant Canis is wearing an appropriately regal ribbon collar, *facing*. Who doesn't love to dress up on occasion? *above left and above right*. Pet collars created out of picot-edged ribbon, ribbon trim, and a lush satin embellished with elegant crystals, *right*.

PULLED ROSE

This ribbon flower is elegant not only in looks but also with the ease in which it is created. It can be used in a multitude of ways, from wardrobe and accessories to home and tabletop décor. It is best made of a wired taffeta, and you can use ribbon that is solid, ombre, iridescent, or even patterned or striped.

Choose a ribbon in a 1-1/2-inch width for this flower, and cut two yards. On one cut end, tie an overhand knot about 1 inch from the end. Moving to the other cut end, pull one wire slightly out on the selvedge of what will be the outside edge of the rosette by about 1 inch. Fold it down to keep it from sliding up into the ribbon as you gather. On the other selvedge, begin to pull the wire out bit by bit and start gathering the ribbon down along its length towards the secured end. This exposes the wire and creates a spiral of ribbon. Continue pulling the wire and gathering the ribbon down its length until you have gathered the ribbon in a spiral of about 18 inches or so. Twist the short exposed wire (ungathered edge) to the long exposed wire and clip away the excess, leaving about 1 inch of secured wire. Take the knotted end of the ribbon in one hand, and with the other hand, start wrapping the gathered ribbon around it, creating a rosette shape. You can use straight pins to secure the rosette underneath as you go. Once the rosette is formed and secured with pins, tack the gathered underside of the flower together with a double-threaded needle, using slightly loose stitches. Work from the center toward the outside, and secure the end by folding it under the flower and tacking it flat. Turn the flower over and arrange the spirals of the rosette to finish.

A selection of handmade ribbon roses, *clockwise from above left:* taffeta fuschias, taffeta poppy, crushed pulled rose, pulled rose, silk folded rose, hatpin rose, and tea rose, *center.*

Love knots can be a simple
way to elevate a bridal bouquet from lovely to
extraordinary while evoking
the glory of brides from the past.

RIBBON *for* WEDDINGS

THERE ARE FEW RITUALS more important in our lives than weddings. At no time are more people so intimately involved in the lives of two individuals than when preparing for, and living, this most romantic of days. Weddings are constants in our society, whose fabric is interwoven with devotion to the ideas of love and courtship. Weddings are a culmination of all the romantic mind can conjure—and they are also big business, with a host of planners, consultants, and coordinators guiding couples every step of the way. Every detail must be perfect, every moment planned.

Ribbons play a valuable part in the look of a wedding, elegantly transforming essential elements of the event such as the invitations, flowers, gowns, and table décor into luxurious visual and tactile treats. Depending on the style or feel desired for the event—classic, romantic, modern, or ethnic—ribbons are perfect for almost every aspect.

REQUEST TO ATTEND

Announcements and invitations that the bride and groom choose set the tone for the event, allowing them to hint at the manner in which their nuptials will be celebrated. Many bridal invitations today, whether custom letterpress, engraved, or embossed, can be embellished with a ribbon in the signature color of the wedding. Store-bought invitations also become more luxurious and personalized with the addition of ribbon. Silk satin is especially popular for this due to its elegance, but organdy, velvet, and taffetas are used as well; a simple wing bow or ribbon border is often all that is needed to "dress" the correspondence.

This vibrant, nontraditional presentation is wonderfully ebullient.

Mr. and Mrs Harris

request the hono...

at the marriage o...

Jennife...

Mr. Ronald...

on Saturday,

Two thou...

at seven...

The Cathe...

Please join us for the
Rehearsal Dinner in honor of

Amanda and Miles

Friday, September 18, 2009
seven o'clock
The Chop Room
Chicago, Illinois

Mary and Harris Anderson

R.s.v.p. 312-478-5175
mary@comcast.com

...e come enjoy swimming, boating and grilling as we celeb...
...emorial Day at the La...
May 29th, 2006
...m. - 10

T he first hint of the style of the event is given in the invitations through the use of color, type of stationery, and font. Here, a superbly styled invitation with delicate script and black picot satin ribbon indicates an evening of exceptional elegance, *facing*. Natural elements paired with ribbon reflect the couples' appreciation for the natural world, *above left*. A bold fuchsia ribbon accentuates the exuberant pattern of the envelope, *above right*. Striped satin lends a tailored look apropos to a formal event, *right*.

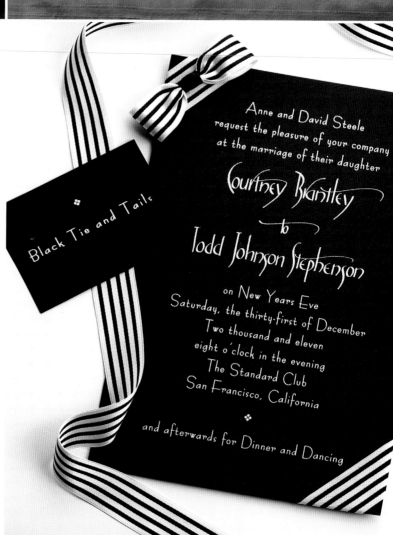

Black Tie and Tails

Anne and David Steele
request the pleasure of your company
at the marriage of their daughter

Courtney Brantley
to
Todd Johnson Stephenson

on New Years Eve
Saturday, the thirty-first of December
Two thousand and eleven
eight o'clock in the evening
The Standard Club
San Francisco, California

and afterwards for Dinner and Dancing

DRESS DETAILS

The bride is a resplendent figure in her wedding finery, which often incorporates ribbon into the design. Sashes are popular again for wedding gowns, and many couture gowns are fantasies of ribbon embellishment with ruching, ribbon embroidery, and ribbon flowers. Corseted gowns crisscrossed with delicate satin ribbon are also in vogue. Ribbon sashes for bridesmaids' gowns or dresses that match the bride's help to connect the dresses visually and in spirit.

A breathtaking arrangement
of ribbon rosettes and vintage millinery items
graces the back of this bridal gown.

Diamonds and champagne: *the sumptuous look* of a jewel-encrusted gown
is lightened with the addition of a soft satin ribbon at the bust, *facing*. A double bow tied at the waist, adorned with a vintage
rhinestone pin, embellishes this gown, *above*.

Veils *and* Headpieces

The bride may choose to pull her hair up and perhaps crown herself with a trio of tuxedo bows accented with jewels, or wear a veil with ribbon trim and millinery flowers or a tiara. Veils can be short or very long, unadorned or embellished with lace, embroidery, beadwork, and ribbon. A sophisticated look we recently gave a bride was a single, delicate burnt ostrich plume in white rising from the back of her upswept hair and beset with a jeweled ribbon rosette.

This delicate burnt-ostrich plume is anchored by a jeweled rosette, creating an elegant vintage look, *above*. The couture bride mixes wide satin ribbon with jewels for her grand entrance, *facing*.

 bride-sophisticate wearing a flirty, delicate veil with satin bows, *facing*. A trio of satin bows crowns the bride, *above left*. Ribbon bands encrusted with jewels evoke a classical look, *above right*. The bride, an impossibly beautiful Renaissance goddess, uses a ribbon as a lush headband accented with a brooch, *right*.

FLORAL ARRANGEMENTS

Helping to impart a sense of celebration and luxury, flowers are of immense importance at weddings, and so careful attention is given to choice and color for arrangements, bouquets, and boutonnieres. Ribbon is a luxurious component for the bride and her bridesmaids' bouquets. Bows and streamers of love knots are traditional ways in which ribbon graces these sweet-smelling items of accoutrement. Wrapping the stems of bouquets with ribbon is not merely decorative: ribbon also helps to hold the flowers together and protect the hands of those who carry them from water or stains. Heavy satin is most often used for this, but velvets and taffetas are also lovely choices. The groom and his men are represented here as well with their diminutive, though no less charming, boutonnieres, often with a tiny satin bow or wrapping.

Embellishing the ribbon on a bouquet with crystal, monograms, or vintage buttons personalizes the bouquet for the bride and her party. There are many embroiderers who will customize ribbon with monograms and special words of personal importance. Monogrammed ribbons can also be used to tie up favor boxes or as embellishment on programs and menus.

Four-inch satin ribbon with crystal marguerites of varying sizes strewn down its length grace this bouquet, *above*. Monogrammed ribbon personalizes the sumptuous bouquet of this refined bride, *right*.

This splendid bride carries a vintage-inspired bouquet complete with love knots, *facing*. Vintage carved shell buttons on the ribbon-wrapped stems of this bouquet are charmingly nostalgic. The handle is finished with a ballet wrap in satins of contrasting color, *above left*. A layered look with exposed stems and a crisp bow is simple and elegant, *above right*. A wide band of gorgeous jacquard is layered over satin in this bouquet. The addition of crystals adds a glimmer of sparkle, *right*.

ibbon accents grace the four handsomely elegant boutonnieres, *facing*, which include *clockwise from top left*: satin ribbon, narrow ombre with a picot edge, iridescent taffeta, and hand-dyed silk. *This page*: Lush velvet in bright green is a simple wrap for this boutonniere, *top left*. Narrow French ombre is used in a mix of real and faux blooms, *top right*. Vintage millinery flowers and fresh leaves are finished with narrow taffeta with a lettuce-edge, *bottom right*.

TABLE SETTINGS

Table settings at weddings are perfect places to continue the use of ribbons, either as ribbon runners that extend lushly to the floor, ribbon bands around vases of flowers or votives, bows tied to hurricanes, or as additional color on place cards. Ribbon napkin rings can be made to match theme or color in many ways with bows, ruching, jeweled drops, vintage and live flowers, or simple rings. Voluptuously large satin bows tied to each chair and left to dangle are not only chic, but also help to spread rich color at a reception dinner. Large trumpet vases towering above the table with streamers of ribbon cascading down are superb decorative elements.

This spectacular table inspired by Chanel in
shell pink and black is a gorgeous example of attention to
detail and grand design, incorporating
ribbons around the base of the arrangement, on the chic
black chairs, and on the table itself.

Cut-crystal bottles dressed with *ribbon bows* are memorable favors for the ladies, *facing*.

The setting: millinery fruits and ribbon napkin rings, *above*.

This vibrant table uses fuchsia, various pinks, and turquoise to enchant guests with rich, saturated color. Four-inch-wide ribbon is tied with a simple bow on every guest's chair for drama and presentation. This setting is rich with color and ribbon details, *left*. Votives and vases are banded with layers of ribbon in related colors and varying textures to please the eye. Shiny blue foil and bright satin ribbon on the favor boxes entice guests, *above right*. Vintage millinery flowers tucked into a simply tied satin ribbon add a touch of elegance and are unique favors for guests, *below right*.

A modern arrangement of branches and orchids presides over this soothing and chic tablescape in vibrant shades of green, *facing*. Whimsical place cards: place settings of simple white linen with a satin ribbon band cushion perfect green apples with paper leaves on which guests' names are inscribed, *above left*. Linen napkins are simply folded and banded with layered ribbon. The gold Dresden leaves play with the use of bare branches from the centerpiece, as if they had just fallen, *above right*. Handmade favor boxes tied with satin ribbon hold delicious chocolates for guests to indulge in, *right*.

THE ULTIMATE CAKE

Without fail at every wedding there is another beauty who effortlessly adds her considerable charm to the event—the wedding cake. The taste, texture, and look of the wedding cake are very important: the cake is one of the things always discussed at one's wedding. Bands of ribbon are one way to make a memorable impression and continue the color or theme of the day. On square or round cakes, ribbon trims in satin or taffeta can be used in inventive ways—tied in bows, made into rosettes and applied to the sides, or cascaded down from a topper of real or sugar flowers. Cakes can be tied up like exquisite gifts and "untied" when ready to cut. Ribbon designs on a cake that match the design details on a bride's gown can be delightful. The cake table might be covered in streamers of ribbon billowing to the floor or cascading down from overhead chandeliers.

The fuchsia embroidery along the edge of the ruched ribbon on this cool green cake is echoed by the vintage millinery leaves cascading down one side in a riot of rich color.

Cupcakes have become popular for weddings and other celebrations in lieu of a single large cake. Here, a fetching group sports ribbon flags in the bride and groom's colors, *above*. Elegant gold satin with an ivory picot overlay sets off the vintage onion roses and velvet leaves of this classic round tier cake, *facing*.

Simple and gorgeous, this ribbon was chosen in the same color as that used on the bride's gown.

The piping is kept to a minimum in order to reflect the couple's spare aesthetic, *facing*. This delightful cake

is adorned with various types of ribbon, some with the addition of a contrasting color and pattern,

adding layers of texture against its smooth white surface, *above*.

FAVORS *and* MORE

The bride and groom thoughtfully choose favors for their guests to take away as a fond remembrance of their new union. The packaging of favors has become a high art, carefully studied and presented with panache. Like most wedding items, favor boxes come in an almost bewildering array of sizes, shapes, and styles. Ribbons are used in many ways to tie or embellish favor boxes, from elegant bows to simple bands of color around the top. Along with ribbon, there might be flowers or buckles on top, natural items like feathers or shells, monograms of beaded wire—basically anything the bride and groom might choose to add a touch of that "extra something" for guests to take away.

In churches, ribbon can be tied to flowers along the pews and to various other floral arrangements or tied in many-looped bows on large candelabras. On the doors of the church or chapel, a set of the couple's initials created out of roses or other blossoms, tied with a simple bow, is a festive way to welcome guests inside.

One of the last scenes from a wedding is the departure of the newly married couple. The getaway vehicle can be traditionally festooned with ribbon streamers and tin cans, both of which announce the happy occasion to the world.

A regal combination of satin ribbon and Dresden crowns. A single crystal jewel on each crown matches the color of the ribbon.

With great packaging, like this ginger tin, all you need is a beautiful velvet bow, *above left*. Favor boxes can be teasingly near-transparent, the ribbon bow hinting at the treat within, *below left*. The creaminess of the satin ribbon and the crisp millinery spray lend themselves to the feeling of simple luxuriousness on this favor box. The flowers are themselves an additional treasure for guests, *right*.

Rich silver foil and vintage crystal buttons accent the soft brown velvet ribbon on this favor box, *above left*. A French bee jacquard is a simple and elegant touch to this chocolate-brown favor box, *above center*. A cluster of exotic parrot feathers and hand-dyed silk ribbon is an unusual and extraordinarily gorgeous presentation, *above right*. Satin picot ribbon adorned with the couple's monogram bands this favor box, *far left*. A simple wrapping of silk cord accents the handsome vintage-style label on this chocolate bar, *left*. Printed ribbon adds a touch of class to this tiny favor box, *right*.

Square sachets created from
taffeta ribbon are tied up with hand-dyed
silk and fine organdy ribbons.

RIBBON IN THE HOME

HOME IS THE PLACE we retreat to from the world for rest and to recharge ourselves daily. It is the place where we entertain, surround ourselves with loved ones, follow the rituals of the seasons, and experience many of life's milestones. It is also a canvas on which we reflect everything we are or aspire to be. The use of ribbons as embellishments helps to make the home luxurious and unique. Ribbon allows for personal expression through extra touches of favorite colors and subtle notes of beauty in otherwise spare interiors. Ribbon can be used to elevate already sumptuous rooms into sanctuaries of luxuriousness.

RIBBON MOTIFS:
FABRICS *and* OBJECTS

In most living areas with soft furnishings, ribbons serve as perfect embellishment accents on upholstery or other fabric goods. Sometimes the ribbon is part of the fabric itself; a classic motif for many fabrics from linen toiles to silk jacquards is ribbons, specifically bows. Many of these designs utilize neoclassical elements and ribbon motifs as part of the overall design of the pattern. Rococo and baroque elements make appearances as well. There is a pedigree: Marie Antoinette's private rooms at Versailles luxuriate in the use of ribbon bows for decorative purposes on furniture, walls, and fabrics. There are innumerable fabrics with ribbon designs available today for any type of fabric use in the home, such as upholstery or drapery. A medium-weight linen with a toile ribbon motif is perfect for a bedroom with French doors; for a living room, one might choose a heavier silk jacquard with a ribbon pattern for elegant drapes or cornices. On the couch, perhaps a silk velvet pillow with embossed ribbon designs undulating across its wonderfully tactile surface can continue the theme.

Ribbon motifs also appear on other items in the home, both decorative and utilitarian, from accessories such as boxes, mirrors, and frames to wood trims with ribbon carvings and wallpaper with ribbon motifs.

Cherished ephemera *gathered up with a ribbon* is not only neatly
kept together, it becomes a new object to admire, *above left*. A charming group of new and
vintage ribbon-motif objects, *above right*. Detail of a toile using ribbon as part of a larger tableau, *below left*.
A jacquard with a ribbon bow and foliage motif, *below right*.

P^{on} 440

10 MÈTRES FIXES

N° 12

Rayonne

This simple mantel *arrangement with a ribbon* motif evokes faded luxuries from the past, *facing*. A vintage ribbon brooch is charming and still fashionable today, *above*.

THE DINING ROOM

In the dining room, chairs with opaque or sheer covers cinched with satin make any luncheon or dinner party an elegant affair. Chandeliers with ribbon sleeves on their cords add another note of elegance. Tablecloths and other table linens can easily be customized with ribbon trims in colors matching upholstered dining chairs, walls, or china. There are dozens of ways in which napkin rings can be made using ribbon. One could stitch a simple ribbon band, tie elegant bows that can be effortlessly untied, layer ribbons, or use ribbon trims. Match the color of ribbon to the china and napkin itself, or go for a surprising contrast in a different yet pleasing color. Other objects tied with or tucked under the ribbon might include chopsticks, vintage millinery flowers and leaves, teardrop crystals, or the unusual, such as small animal horns for an exotic-themed dinner. Place cards embellished with ribbon are a nice personal touch, and they can also bring color to the table with the choice of colored card stock and bright ribbons. Personalizing wine or champagne stems with various-colored ribbon bows is a thoughtful way to help guests keep track of drinks during parties.

Votives for the table can be banded with ribbon, and impressive candelabras might be dressed with large, soft bows in silk taffeta that glow in the warm light.

Candles present the perfect object for ribbon adornment; the ribbons glow when the candles are lit, *left*. The grandeur of this antique crystal candelabra is softened by the rich pink color of a taffeta bow, *facing*.

An enchanting assemblage of avian treasures
from the natural world is accented with a beautiful ribbon, *facing*.
For an aromatic centerpiece, create a pyramid of fresh lemons
by using toothpicks to keep them together. Top with a luxurious
taffeta ribbon in tropical colors, *above*.

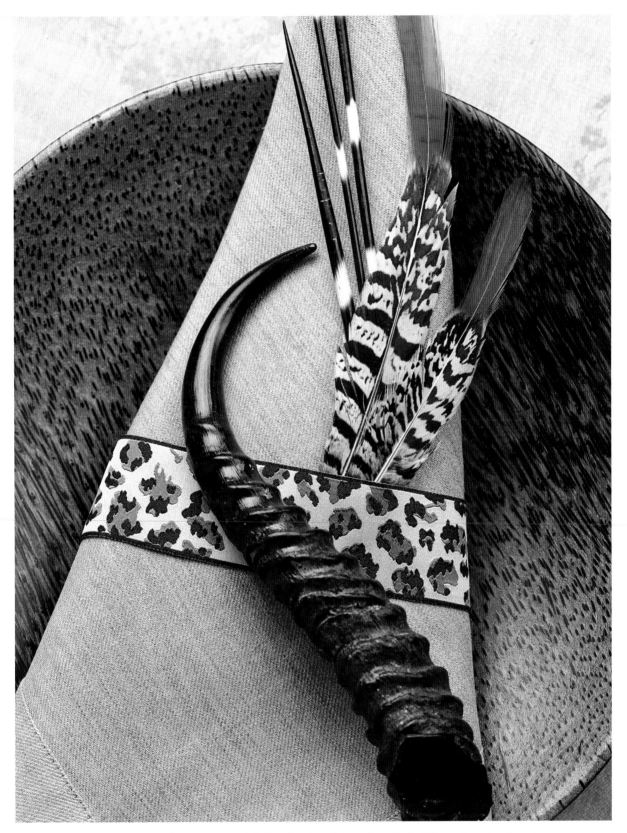

Facing page, clockwise from top left: A striped and dotted ruched ribbon ring stands out against a simple, graphic setting; a speckled quail's egg and narrow silk ribbon bands evoke brunch at a French country house; a trio of millinery leaves accented with taffeta for a fall buffet; inspirations for a table setting. Out of Africa: bring the exotic to the table with animal print ribbons and beautiful horns, quills, and feathers, *above*.

stylish luncheon or dinner requires beautiful china, exceptional silver, and gorgeous napkin rings of ribbon, *this page and facing.*

he saturated color of these millinery flowers and the accompanying variegated ribbon serves to enhance the appeal of the vintage transferware china, *facing*. A lovely variegated ribbon brightens a teatime setting, *above left*. Sheer glamour graces this place setting in the form of satin ribbon bands on the napkins with a crystal droplet reminiscent of a diamond choker, *above right*. Stems for guests are given individual ribbons as an elegant way to keep track of drinks at gatherings, *right*.

Tucking fresh herbs into ribbon napkin rings is a simple way to add texture and a lovely scent to the table, *above*.

A napkin ring of striped taffeta ribbon echoes the angle of the napkin's fold in this appealing setting, *facing*.

THE BEDROOM

Privacy reigns in the bedroom, and one can luxuriate there in the quiet interiors where we spend a large part of our lives. Naturally, the more luxurious, the better. Bed linens are perfect for ribbon embellishment, such as satin or grosgrain bands on crisp white duvets or narrow satin threaded on hemstitched pillows and shams. Pillowcases and sheets can be personalized with ribbon edging. Hanging bed linens might be tied to bedposts with crisp taffeta bows and delicate dressing table chairs embellished with soft hanging bows and long tails just grazing the floor.

Children's rooms are places of daydreams and fantasy. Ribbon can be used to brighten these rooms and to foster creativity when used in inventive ways, such as outlining doors and windows with grosgrain or streaming wide, colorful ribbons in canopies over beds. For girls, choose ribbons such as delicate pastel organdies, shiny satins, and whimsical polka-dot grosgrains. Boys should have taffetas, solid or striped (as in a nautical theme) grosgrains, and heavier textured novelty ribbons.

These pillows are tied up with ribbons and bows but look no less smashing for the simplicity of the embellishment.

Tied up with ribbon,
towels and bath linens presented
for guests impart a
"bed and breakfast" feel, *facing.*

THE BATHROOM

In the bathroom and powder room, hand towels and other bath linens can be decorated with ribbon trim like satin or grosgrain to match walls and tile. Stitching a ribbon border along the hem or valance of a shower curtain can literally transform it. Tissue boxes and small trash bins are good articles for a luxe band of ribbon. Tie soaps with a lovely satin ribbon and pile them on a small pedestal plate or tray by the sink. For overnight guests, a basket of wrapped soaps and toiletries, along with a small box of chocolates sporting a pretty ribbon, adds a thoughtful note of comfort.

Fine bath
linens can be customized by
adding borders of ribbon that
match the theme or colors of
the bathroom, *left.*

Everyday Objects

Various objects and accessories in the home can be embellished or their use enhanced by ribbon. Old keys still in use—such as those for china cabinets and rooms in old houses—are lovely when hung from various ribbons. Books can be tied up with ribbon and placed on a reading table or coffee table, or each volume may have its own ribbon bookmark. Favorite letters and vintage correspondence can be embellished with ribbon and placed on a shelf, mantel, or bulletin board. *Objets d'art* such as a bust or sculpture can be embellished with ribbon for a touch of whimsy. Such favorite assemblages as a compote holding a still life of a bird's nest and eggs are places to use ribbons.

Vases of flowers with coordinating ribbon are at home in any room of the house, and sachets stitched from wide ribbon and tied up with bias-cut silk ribbon are a delightful find in a drawer or on a closet shelf. The classic French sachets of woven lavender stems use satin in their design, making them not only fragrantly functional but also beautiful.

Ribbons woven in patterns such as argyle or harlequin on pillows are colorful accents for otherwise staid pieces of furniture. Pillows can also be dressed up by simply tying them up like a package with a neat bow.

A casually arranged tableau of
vintage objects is paired with ribbons.

ookmarks are a classic —and smart—way to utilize extra lengths of ribbon too small to use otherwise but too lovely to toss out, *facing*. The past captured: old skeleton keys are tied up with a ribbon bow, enhancing their timeworn charm, *above and right*.

These sachets are handmade with *wide taffeta ribbon* and filled with fresh lavender, *above*.

Ribbons tied around these modern vases unify the various flowers and textures, *facing*.

DRAPERY TREATMENTS

Window treatments in any room of the home can be customized with ribbon trim. Tie-backs of ribbon and ribbon cockades are nice alternatives to typical braided tiebacks. Cornices with ruched ribbon along their sculptural edges are quietly sumptuous. Simple streamers of silk or organdy ribbon hanging to the floor in front of a sheer panel glow when the sun enters. Soft linen panels might be given a tailored look by adding bands of pleated silk taffeta at the hem in a neutral color or perhaps a vibrant shade for contrast. There are innumerable drapery fabrics and styles of window treatments to which ribbons and trims can be added.

Lamp Shades *and* Cords

Lamp shades can be trimmed with narrow satin ribbons or delicate rococo trims. Ribbons can be applied vertically or in bands that encircle the shade. For a feminine look, especially for a young girl's room, large, soft satin bows tied around shades with long flirty tails are charming. A library might have a reading lamp whose shade is embellished with ribbons in a plaid pattern. Pendant lights and chandeliers assume a custom look with velvet ribbon sleeves.

Dressing electrical cords on lamps and chandelier chains with ribbon sleeves imparts a tailored look to any room, and it couldn't be simpler to create. Satin, velvet, or taffeta ribbon adds just the right note of luxury.

Choose a ribbon that is either 1-1/2 inches wide or 4 inches wide, depending on the size of the cord or chain to be covered. The length of the ribbon should be 1-1/2 times the length of the cord for ruching; for a more lush look, use 3 times the length.

If using 1-1/2-inch-wide ribbon, cut two equal lengths and place them face to face. Stitch along both selvedges, leaving the ends open. When finished, turn the sleeve inside out by attaching a safety pin at one end and pulling it through bit by bit.

If you are using a 4-inch ribbon, simply fold one length of ribbon selvedge to selvedge face in and stitch along the open side, making a tube. Use a safety pin to turn the sleeve right side out by pinning it at one end and inverting the sleeve over it, moving it along inside with your fingers. Slide the finished sleeve over the cord or chain and tuck the ends in (you can finish the ends by gluing or stitching if you prefer). Arrange the ruching evenly.

Iridescent taffeta is used to
create a shimmering, sinuous cord sleeve.

BULLETIN BOARDS

Staying organized is something everyone aspires to, and in the home one should practice this as much as possible so that clutter doesn't rule. One way in which this can be accomplished with mail, photos, notes, postcards, recipes, children's drawings, and a host of other items one wants to hold onto or view on a regular basis is the bulletin board.

Bulletin boards are perfect not only for organizational purposes but also as decorative elements in the home. Adapting them to the room or a particular use is done with choice of color, fabric, and ribbon. They can be large or diminutive and also covered in paper, such as maps or patterned paper. Alternatively, the cork can also be left exposed and then adorned with ribbon. Heavier satins, ribbon trims, and grosgrains are perfect choices for holding items to the surface of the board. Create a crisscross or square pattern across the width of the board, attaching it to the back with staples or tacks and glue. Use decorative tacks at the intersection of each ribbon on the front to allow items to be tucked into the ribbon. Very large boards can be hinged together to create a standing screen or room divider. Theme boards can be inspiring, using ideas such as art, cooking, sports, vintage ephemera, and so on. Choosing to create a board in certain colors to match a room or décor (such as the kitchen or a child's room) makes it even more special. We often choose a theme for a board in projects we are working on, which allows it to serve as inspiration and a vertical working surface for sketches, swatches, and other related items.

Large French bulletin boards allow one to create and arrange various assemblages of photos, ephemera, and other objects to provide inspiration for the home, office, or studio.

Yves Saint Laurent
David Teboul

CHANEL and her world
Charles Roux

TIMELESS TIARAS

SO FAR SO GOUDE

THE CENTURY OF THE DESIGNER

THE EVENING DRESS · BLACK

Paris De Luxe · PLACE V

LES GIRLS

This bulletin board, inspired by Elsa Schiaparelli's
Shocking Pink, combines fashion and a touch of the whimsical on a board with lively fabric
and jet ribbon, *facing*. Inspiring as any fine painting, this French bulletin board of collected
ephemera tells stories through the objects themselves, *above*.

La Mode Illustrée

*Details of the prints
are rendered three-dimensional
by the addition of ribbon and
padding, left.*

Pictures *and* Art

Ribbon can also be used as art in the home. Exceptional vintage ribbon work, swatch cards, or just lovely pieces of old ribbon can be matted and framed. Art and framed photographs hung by ribbon surmounted by bows or cockades is classic and an ideal way to introduce another element of color to enhance any room's décor.

Vintage articles of clothing with ribbon work can be placed on new or vintage dress forms (or padded hangers, even) and placed as sculptural pieces in a room. Millinery items are perfect on wired or wooden hat stands or, even better, on vintage hat blocks. An assortment of old military medals on a vintage officer's jacket is a great way to display such a collection and add atmosphere to a library or boy's room.

*Vintage ladies' fashion book
prints embellished with ribbon
and framed, facing.*

LA MODE ILLUSTRÉE

A large double cockade is a perfect ornamental detail for this antique photograph and gently worn frame of a group of gentlemen, *above*. A piece of vintage ribbon trim is matted and framed, then surmounted by a rosette of rich taffeta ribbon, *below*. Various ribbons and trims can be framed and matted landscape-style to hang as inspiring art, *facing*.

Create festive party hats by
spraying paper hats with a fixative glue and
covering in fabric or paper. Add
ribbon in the form of pom-poms or flowers,
ruffled trims along the bottom,
narrow ribbon applied around the hat's
circumference, and as ties.

CELEBRATIONS *and*
SEASONAL EMBELLISHMENTS

THE PASSAGE OF TIME in our lives is marked by celebrations and the seasons. Everyone adores parties and sharing in festive celebrations together. Each year is filled with birthdays, anniversaries, baby and wedding showers, bachelor and bachelorette parties, bar and bat mitzvahs, and graduations. Each holiday we give and attend many parties.

We give and receive gifts, we dress up, and we decorate our homes for our guests and ourselves. Ribbons are one of many important elements of the celebrations and holidays we all take part in, especially when giving gifts and decorating our homes.

GIFT PRESENTATION

Part of special celebrations such as birthdays and holidays like Christmas is giving gifts. The way in which one presents gifts is part of the gift itself, and whether you focus on specific colors, a theme for the celebration, or holiday décor, using ribbon enhances the charm of the gift and says you care enough to pay attention to detail.

Start with the paper, and then choose your ribbons and any accents or small favors for the outside of the box. The variety of papers available today for giftwrapping in general is outstanding. We love the traditional foil papers that are available in a variety of colors and designs. Old-fashioned printed papers with birthday and holiday themes never lose their charm; unwired taffetas and satins pair well with these papers. Flocked paper in large sheets or on rolls is available for sumptuous presentations of rich colors on plain or metallic backgrounds. For impressive papers like these, contrast the richness with a smooth satin ribbon or taffeta tied into a simple bow. For multiple gifts, choose another paper, a solid in a complementary color with a smooth finish to wrap other packages with, and use a velvet ribbon. Presented together, the effect will be stunning.

Contemporary printed or silkscreened papers, even artist's papers, can be used as well for any celebration. Some of the best papers available have patterns like houndstooth, paisley, stripes, circles, and even antique calligraphy. There are papers available with metallic glittered designs and lovely Japanese papers with intricate silkscreened designs. Imagine a black or red satin ribbon tied obi-style around a beautifully

The ribbons chosen here perfectly accent the paper and additional embellishments—natural elements, a large Dresden letter, and a spray of millinery leaves—on each gift.

wrapped box. Jeweled buckles can be used as a sophisticated way to add ribbon to a package; simply wrap the ribbon around the box like a belt and slide the ends through the buckle.

Gift presentation can be exceptional even when utilitarian papers such as Kraft or newsprint are used by pairing them with contrastingly rich ribbons. A gorgeous holiday theme we recently created was a woodland Christmas. We paired plain Kraft paper on the packages with a rich red and green taffeta and various grosgrains in nature's colors. On each package we attached a spray of vintage cotton millinery mushrooms or pinecones and branches. For a late October birthday party, the use of Kraft paper with a rich chocolate taffeta and other fall embellishments would be appropriate and a nice departure from the usual birthday wrappings.

For gift giving, there are no hard-and-fast rules save that you take your time to wrap each present as well as you can; it's not a disaster if a little tape shows on your package (using double-sided tape helps), but there should never be any tears or rips in the paper. If at all possible, try to keep the corners crisp and the edges smooth. Anything of an unusual shape or size should go into a box large enough to accommodate it.

GIFTWRAP SUPPLIES

It's always good to keep a few supplies on hand for last-minute gifts (such as a hostess gift) or simply to be prepared for any occasion by stocking up on any beautiful papers, ribbons, favors, and other ephemera one might use for gifts. Below is a general list of items we find helpful to keep on hand as part of your giftwrap supplies.

RIBBON: Be sure to keep on hand a variety of ribbons such as satins, grosgrains, taffetas, and trims of good quality in various colors and widths.

PAPER SHEARS: Keep your paper shears well sharpened; use them only for cutting paper.

RIBBON SHEARS: We use dressmaker's shears to cut our ribbon, along with a quality pair of pinking shears for decorative cuts.

TAPE: Regular Scotch tape and double-sided tape are both essentials.

GIFTWRAP AND VARIOUS PAPERS: Purchase both rolls and loose sheets of various patterns for different occasions. We love beautiful papers and are always on the lookout for something new and unique.

TISSUE PAPER: We love to use tissue paper inside boxes. Keep several colors on hand, especially white or ivory.

BOXES: Keep various shapes and sizes on hand so that you will have the right size when needed. Remember when purchasing a gift that boxes are usually available from the merchant in the correct size, if you choose to use one of theirs.

 number of elements make this gift presentation superb: a beautiful paper, millinery flowers tucked in for enhancement as well as for an extra favor, and coordinating ribbon tied into a simple bow, *above left*. Various exquisite papers matched up with the perfect ribbons, *above right*. An elegant, feminine selection of papers, ribbons, and favors, *right*.

EASTER CLASSICS

The classic Easter basket is every child's dream conveyance for brightly colored eggs and chocolate bunnies. Ribbons are perfectly suited for these, tied in bright colorful bows on the handles or around the basket or pail itself. Taffetas, satins, and especially organdies are perfect. A spray of vintage millinery violets, lily of the valley, or other spring silk flowers tucked under ribbon that has been wound around the handle is beautiful. Different colors of ribbon help to identify each basket for its excited young owner.

The Easter basket can also be used as a decorative item in the home. A mound of painted or dyed eggs nestled in pastel grass is the classic image of Easter. A lovely variation of this is a simple basket of brown hen's eggs or diminutive speckled quail eggs with natural buff-colored grass. A pale ivory or soft blue satin ribbon tied in a simple bow on the handle is all that's needed to evoke a less colorful but no less charming appreciation of spring. Another idea for displaying white or dyed eggs is to hot-glue 3/8-inch bands of velvet or satin ribbon around their circumference.

Easter trees are more recent additions to the holiday, hung with jellied candies and ornaments. Use satin ribbon to hang hollowed pastel eggs from bare branches along with vintage Easter postcards and ornaments.

Another Easter staple is the Easter dress, along with a new hat or bonnet, for young girls and babies. Ribbon sashes trailing elegantly from silk and organdy dresses are a lovely sight. If a dress comes without ribbon, look for a silk satin in the right color to use as a sash or to attach to a simple portrait hat with a flower. A plain bonnet can be embellished with ribbon as well as small silk flowers, vintage or new.

This Easter basket features an arrangement of vintage flowers and postcards topped by an extravagant bow of taffeta ribbons, one of which is printed with colorful birds.

In this breathtaking basket, *colorful eggs nestle* in moss among diminutive
posies, and velvet violets are tucked into the striped taffeta ribbon winding up the handle, *facing*. A chocolate bunny
wears his Easter finery in the form of a crisp plaid ribbon, *above*.

HALLOWEEN

Fall arrives with crisp nights and cool days of gorgeous color. Summer is gone, the harvest is in, and ghosts prowl the streets. Partygoers and trick-or-treaters celebrate the holiday that is second only to Christmas in the United States in terms of popularity and money spent. Ribbons, especially in black, orange, and white, are perfect for evoking the spooky spirit of the holiday when used on costumes, as streamers, as ties on deliciously filled goody bags, on invitations, and even on pumpkins. A group of pumpkins and strange-looking gourds, each with its own jaunty taffeta bow gathered on a side table or stair step, is a nice holiday accent. Hurricanes with black candles and orange satin bows, or vice versa, are a striking and elegant part of table décor.

Something we do every year is purchase vinyl mice and faux ravens at our local party store. We cover the mice in black glass glitter and adorn with new crystal eyes and bows, while the ravens each get a bow with a jeweled drop. Items covered in glass glitter should never be given to children, but these are perfect as takeaways or favors for adult party guests.

A date for the ball: this duo of masks is adorned with stripes of contrasting velvet ribbon, crystal jewels, and millinery leaves, *above*. These mice, covered in German glass glitter, fancy themselves a glamorous "rat pack" when attired in diminutive ribbon bows as they gather on a silver cake stand, *facing*.

Halloween presents many opportunities to use ribbon for favors
and party décor. Cellophane bags of candy are perfect for tying up with a ribbon in the colors of the season,
facing. Holiday spectator: this charming handcrafted kitty sports a simple
satin bow and insouciantly stands watch over the festivities from under her dome, *above*.

THE MAGIC of CHRISTMAS

These are the things of Christmas: gift giving, trees, wreaths, stockings, snow, mystery and enchantment, liturgical and popular holiday music, sumptuous dinners with family and friends, the smell of evergreens and bayberry, quiet moments of joy on Christmas Eve, and ecstatic mayhem on Christmas morning.

The traditional colors of the season—red, green, and white (along with gold and silver)—make the holiday a rich and sparkling pageant of color. Many people don't realize the significance of the original Christmas colors or their origin. The colors are actually inspired by a species of mushroom that is deeply rooted in Germanic folklore, called *Amanita muscaria*, or fly agaric. The mushrooms, sporting bright red caps dotted with irregular white spots, appear under evergreen trees in northern Europe (as well as North America) during the bleak winter months. Poisonous and extremely hallucinogenic, *Amanita muscaria* was once used by shamans for various rituals. Over the ages, as the traditions of the pagan world merged with those of the new Christian world, these colors became emblematic of the season, as did the Christmas tree and Santa Claus.

The Christmas tree is the perfect place to use voluminous garlands of ribbon either cascading down the branches in long streamers or in the more traditional manner of swags encircling the tree. Instead of a star or angel, try a magnificent multilooped bow at the top and allow the ribbon streamers to flow downward from

A delicate scrolled text is
printed on the silver ribbon chosen for this wreath
of vintage lacquered and glittered holly leaves.

it. The best width of ribbon to use for medium-to-large-sized trees is 2-1/2 inches. For very large trees, a 3-inch-or-more width is preferred. Small trees look better with 1 to 1-1/2-inch widths. Wired taffeta, satin, or velvet ribbons are used for trees and garlands. There are many quality ribbons with designs for the season either woven in or printed on the ribbon. Patterns or solids can be used separately or together depending on your colors and theme, if any.

A great idea that we put to good use is the ribbon chain, our version of the old-fashioned paper chain made by generations of children. We use wired taffeta in various matching colors to make loops instead of paper. For another variation of traditional Christmas décor, hang ornaments from branches with ribbon instead of hooks. Or perhaps hang a select few with ribbon: very special heirloom or expensive ornaments can be hung with a narrow satin or velvet ribbon surmounted by a small bow.

Garlands and wreaths have always been decorated with ribbon. A traditional wreath of mixed evergreens is somewhat bland without the dashing color afforded by a ribbon embellishment. Wreaths can be hung by ribbon, bows can be attached to the wreath itself, or one can wind ribbon about the wreath. One wreath we created was made of bare branches covered in white plaster and then painted and coated in glass glitter. A silky, intense red satin ribbon, attached as a bow to the wreath, was the only thing needed to finish it perfectly. Greens on mantels and over doors should be accented with streamers of ribbon meandering in and amongst the branches to give them depth and add to their festive charm. Stockings look great hung with ribbon trailing down their length.

The traditions of Christmas are wonderful, but no one should feel constrained by them; why not use different ideas in décor that don't follow the same rules? Go with unconventional themes or colors if you choose—or update the classic green and red with vibrant ribbons and trims to make the season memorable.

hough pinecone wreaths are classics of the season, people often keep them up all year. A wide taffeta ribbon with a plaid stripe down its center adds a bright burst of color and draws out the warmer tones in the natural material, *above left*. A woodland wreath hanging attractively from a plaid taffeta ribbon is dressed beautifully for the holidays, *above right*. This pussy willow wreath can be used any time of year. The wide ombre striped taffeta adds color and movement, *right*.

Vibrant blue satin ribbon pairs well with the pewter-colored balls composing this attractive wreath. A large Chinese silk millinery flower is centered above the bow for an extra touch of extravagance, *above*. Holly Golightly's holiday fantasy: this sparkling wreath of vintage brooches and beaded embellishments is a dream of holiday glamour realized. A soft satin ribbon in platinum crowns the jeweled masterpiece, *facing*.

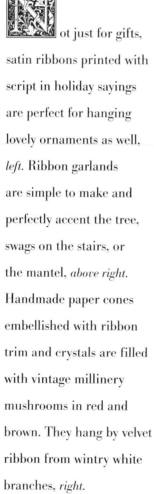

Not just for gifts, satin ribbons printed with script in holiday sayings are perfect for hanging lovely ornaments as well, *left*. Ribbon garlands are simple to make and perfectly accent the tree, swags on the stairs, or the mantel, *above right*. Handmade paper cones embellished with ribbon trim and crystals are filled with vintage millinery mushrooms in red and brown. They hang by velvet ribbon from wintry white branches, *right*.

PORTFOLIO

I LOVE TO FLEX my creative muscles with new ideas and projects either for myself or others. Nicholas Kniel the boutique is a fertile ground for creative endeavors, especially with all the wonderful ribbons and vintage items we've been able to collect together. Often we will find ourselves in an impromptu, spontaneous creative collaboration with a client who needs help with a gown, costume, or event. Many times we choose to pursue projects with nothing more in mind than simply exploring the possibilities afforded by ribbons and anything we chance to come across that we adore. The results often find themselves displayed in the store, helping to foster ideas for others while serving as visual treats for everyone. The boutique is truly like an atelier in this way.

Recently I found myself musing over the concept of the modern woman and dress and how that concept has changed over time. I always smile when women tell me they can't wear a dress with a ribbon flower or sash or a simple bow in their hair. They are too busy with work, children, and life to "dress up." I think of my maternal grandmother, a widow raising six children and working as an executive secretary,

who always dressed flawlessly with perfect hair and makeup like all women of her era. Our world today is certainly more complicated than hers, but sometimes those extra feminine details can make all the difference in how we feel about ourselves and what we present to the world. I decided to do a tongue-in-cheek photo shoot showing the idea of yesterday's "perfect woman" as sexy siren, superb hostess, seductive showgirl, and "perfectly sculpted" gardener.

Frequently we collaborate with other organizations on projects. One of our favorite ongoing collaborations is with *The Atlanta Ballet*. Several years ago, our friend Gailen, who is a great supporter of the ballet, asked us to join her in decorating used pointe shoes to sell as a fundraising venture for the ballet. We have always loved the ballet ourselves and so we were delighted to participate. I did four pairs of pointe shoes and Timothy did four, choosing various colors and themes and using lots of ribbon, vintage flowers and crystals, and fabrics. Each one was a unique work of art. They were a huge hit, and we ended up doing the pointe shoes as centerpieces for the Ballet Ball that year, raising a fair amount of money—all but a few of the pointe shoes sold before anyone was even seated for dinner. Over the years we've continued to collaborate with the ballet, culminating with the creation of masks and miniature mannequins in ballet dress as centerpieces for the Seventy-fifth Anniversary Ball.

A simple tableau
of ribbon, old jewelry, and vintage sewing
items arranged on a platter
and a small cake stand provides a visual
means of inspiration.

WORKING *with* RIBBON

CREATING PROJECTS WITH ribbon is a wonderful way to express your personality and explore your artistic talents. The more one handles ribbon, the more one becomes aware of its properties and the great potential it has for transforming anything into something fantastic. Ribbon is inspiring. Hold it up to the light and examine the sheen, texture, or pattern. Pin it to a dress form or the wall in graceful swags. Drape it or pile it up and let your imagination go. With the information in this chapter on how to work with various ribbon trims and bows, tips on storage and care, and more inspirational ideas, we hope you will be further inspired to create and find new ways to use ribbon in your own unique projects.

RIBBON MANIPULATION

There are many ways in which ribbon is manipulated to create a new design or trim. One can sew, glue, or press ribbon, add other elements such as beads or embroidery to it, or even combine a number of ribbons for new looks.

Bows: Lengths of ribbon can be tied or stitched into various looped designs for this most widely used method of decoratively holding things together or closed. It is also a highly popular motif in design.

Box pleated: Most ribbon is suited to the symmetrically pleated and tacked design of the classic box pleat.

Covered buttons: A variety of ribbons are suited to covering buttons, including taffeta, silk, and velvet. It is very easy to cover a button with ribbon, provided you have the right width of ribbon for the button. Kits for covering buttons are available at craft or fabric stores.

Crushed: This ribbon is water-treated and crushed while wet, giving it a crinkled, distressed look. Perfect for vintage-style designs.

Dyeing: Ribbons of natural fibers, such as silk, rayon, and cotton, can be hand-dyed for custom applications.

Flowers: Ribbons can be manipulated to create a number of incredibly realistic or fantasy flowers for use on everything from clothing to home accessories.

Various manipulated ribbon trims create a rich
still life of texture and color.

Frayed: Frayed ribbon is clipped and the threads pulled along the edges, creating a fringe. In the case of bias-cut silk ribbon, the selvedges are drawn along a knife or scissors blade to create a feathery edge.

Knitted/braided: Various ribbons knitted or plaited together to create a single new design.

Pleated: Pleated ribbon has continuous pressed folds down its length, giving it an accordion-like effect. This can be done by hand or by machine.

Ruching: From the old French *ruche,* meaning "beehive." With this technique, ribbon is stitched and gathered along the edges or down the center, creating a ruffled look. This is a quick and easy way to create a ribbon trim.

Serpentine: Stitched in a zigzag pattern, ribbon is then gathered to create an undulating trim similar to ricrac.

Ribbon-covered buttons are piled below frayed silk and taffeta and knitted silk ribbon, *above*. Knitted silk ribbon features soft variations of color, *facing*.

RIBBON EMBELLISHMENT

Though ribbon itself is an embellishment, it too can be embellished, taking the presentation one step further. This allows one to create entirely new trims for specific projects, such as a vintage-style beaded velvet choker or layered ribbons on a special package for a luxe look.

Appliqué: This technique, popular in many sewing disciplines, is used to create rich or whimsical new designs by adding such things as lace, bouillon appliqués, or embroidered and beaded trims. These can either be tacked or glued to the length of the ribbon.

Crystal flatbacks and beads: Flatback crystals can be used along with various types of beads to embellish ribbon. These can also be tacked or glued as necessary to create exceptional jewelry, such as chokers, or fanciful trims for luxurious effect. Swarovski makes a fine array of crystal flatbacks and beads.

Ribbon layering: Ribbons can easily be layered over one another to create new designs. For instance, one might make a trim by centering a narrow velvet ribbon down the length of a wide satin ribbon of contrasting color.

Monograms: Monograms can be added to ribbons for a classic, personal touch.

Printing: Ribbons can be custom printed with a variety of designs, or a stamp and fabric paint can easily be used to create one's own design.

Various elegant embellished ribbons,
including monogrammed, printed, and appliquéd
with crystals, nestle in a silver tray.

NKE
John and Donna
8.15.09
LE LOUVRE
NÔTRE - DAME
PLACE VENDÔME
RIVE GAUCHE
London · Paris · New York
Félicitations

RIBBON FINISHING

It is important to finish the ends of any ribbon so that the final look is clean and neat.

45-degree-angle straight cut: This is a simple angled cut, leaving one selvedge longer than the opposing selvedge of the ribbon.

Buttons: Buttons, particularly unusual or vintage ones in contrasting colors, are a perfect way to finish the ends of ribbon by sewing one or two back-to-back on each raw end.

Decorative cuts: There are a number of scissors and rotary blades available today that one can use to give ribbon ends more elaborate cuts, many reminiscent of the Victorian era.

Dovetail and double dovetail: The most ubiquitous of cuts for ribbon, this is a deep inverted "V" and is a classic, formal look. The double dovetail is simply two sets of dovetail cuts that give the appearance of a giant pinked edge.

Leaves: New or vintage velvet millinery leaves can be attached to the ends of ribbons for a unique look.

Pinked: Traditional pinking shears give ribbon ends a crisp, classic appearance.

Points: The two corners of the raw end of the ribbon can be tacked together and a bead added to create a point.

Scalloped: Like the undulating curves of the scallop shell after which it is named, this decorative effect is created with a rotary blade, creating a nice alternative to the crisp lines of a pinked edge.

Sumptuous ribbon place markers add
to the pleasure of a good book.

Ribbon Weaving

Various ribbons can be woven together to create patterns for the embellishment of such items as pillows or place mats.

Stripe: These are bands of ribbon in two or more alternating colors that do not overlap. Stripes can be vertical, horizontal, or angled, *facing*.

Plain: Two colors of ribbon that intersect one over the other at right angles create contrasting squares of color similar to a checkerboard, *above left*.

Harlequin: This diamond pattern is made of intersecting ribbons in two or three colors of the same width, after the costume of the classic comic character in the Italian commedia dell'arte, *above right*.

Argyle: This is a square-within-square pattern of intersecting ribbons in several colors and widths turned at an angle. Argyle is derived from the pattern of the tartan of the Argyll clan of Scotland, *right*.

RIBBON BOWS

The one thing everyone thinks of when regarding ribbon is the bow. These lovely and practical embellishments come in a multitude of variations. In fact, one could write an entire book on the bow and different tying techniques alone. Different types of ribbon create different looks for bows. Consider a tuxedo bow tied with both satin and velvet. The former is classic, the latter a quirky vintage look. Bows are more secure if stitched and often look more tailored that way, whereas hand-tied bows are lusher and can be deliciously pulled open.

Multiloop: This bow can have four or six full loops that are centered over the knot for a more luxurious presentation. It is perfect for wreaths or packages. To make a multilooped bow, begin by either laying the ribbon down flat with the right end in front of you or holding the right end in your right hand. The right end of the ribbon will be the center of the bow. With your left hand, fold over a length of ribbon to meet at the right end of the ribbon (the center of the bow). This creates one left loop. Create a right loop in the same way, making sure it is the same size as the left loop. Continue making loops this way, essentially folding the ribbon accordion-style. Fold as many times as you want loops. You can keep the folds the same length, or make them slightly smaller as you go along so that there are longer loops at the outside of the bow and smaller ones in towards the center. Make sure to vary the size every two folds only so each loop has a matching mate. When all the folds are made, pinch them together at the very center, and tie a second length of ribbon over them to cinch them together. This center ribbon will also serve as the tails, but if you already have

Glamorous detail: a smooth satin bow presents a harmonious contrast with the glittering texture of a wreath composed of new and vintage jewelry.

tails from making the loops, you can trim away the excess. You can also use florist's wire to pinch the center together if you are going to use the ribbon on a wreath or tree; add a length of ribbon for tails if needed, and use the wire to attach the bow.

Tuxedo: An elegant bow with two flattened loops and a small center knot with no tails, this is the classic style men wear with tuxedos, hence the name. For projects, it is best stitched and then applied, rather than tied in the classic style. Start by taking a small length of ribbon and fold it over on itself. Stitch the raw ends together and gather them to create one loop, or side, of the bow. The size of the bow is determined by the loops, so you can adjust the size of the loops by trimming away any excess ribbon or using a single piece that, when folded, will make the desired-size loop. Create two loops and stitch them together at the gathered raw ends. Take another small length of the same ribbon and wrap it over the center, then stitch the ends on the reverse to hold it in place.

Single bow: The original bow, still the most classic, has two loops on either side of a center knot and tails. This one can also be stitched or left loose to be pulled open. Form a single loop at the center of the ribbon while holding the ribbon in your fingers. Wrap the longer end of the ribbon around the loop, creating another loop and pulling it through at the same time, just as you would when tying your shoe. Adjust the size of the loops by pulling on them to make them larger; you can reduce the size of the loops by pulling on the tails. Trim the tails to make them even. If you are making a single bow that is not tied to a package or other item, use a small dowel or a pencil as a base on which to tie the bow.

Stacked bow: Two tuxedo bows, one smaller than the other, are stacked together to create this bow. Make two tuxedo bows, one larger than the other. Place the smaller bow over the center of the larger one, aligning them so that they are evenly stacked. Tack or use glue to hold them together before using as embellishment.

Wing bow: Rather than loops, a wing bow has a center knot and two lengths of ribbon cut at a 45-degree angle on either side, like wings. These bows are simple to make yet elegant for any number of projects. Take a length of ribbon two inches longer than the desired width of the finished bow and tie a knot in the center. Keep the knot slightly loose, rather than pulling it tight; this keeps it from being too small in the center. Flatten out the ribbon on either side of the knot and trim the ends at a 45-degree angle, both in the same direction. You can also trim the ends straight, pink them, or give them dovetails.

CARING *for* FINE RIBBON

Fine ribbon, if cared for properly, will last indefinitely. There are many techniques and secrets for keeping ribbons and other fine textiles clean and protected from the ravages of use and time. Everyone swears by this method or that, but we find the best methods are usually the simplest, as are the ones below.

❧ For stained or dingy ribbon, first remove surface dust by blowing or lightly brushing it away. Hand wash with a mild laundry detergent made specifically for delicate items; air dry. Never use any kind of bleach on ribbon.

❧ Vintage ribbon often needs just a light dusting to remove debris accumulated over time, but if you must wash, do so gently by soaking the ribbon in a very mild detergent and carefully rinse. Keep in mind the fragility of older textiles, never wringing them and making sure to lay them flat to air-dry out of the sun.

❧ To press ribbon that is wrinkled, use a pressing cloth and a low iron setting. A bit of gentle steam helps. Be mindful of the types of fibers you are working with and their age. Cotton takes an iron better than silk, but vintage cotton may be more fragile than a new silk ribbon.

❧ Sometimes there are items with ribbon embellishments such as flowers and trims that need attention—old hats in particular can collect dust in crevices. The best method to remove the surface dirt from items like this is to take a panty hose or fine sock and place it over the nozzle of the long-arm attachment of a vacuum. Take care to secure it tightly with

a rubber band. Turn on the vacuum and gently go over the dusty areas of the item, being careful not to press the nozzle too closely to the ribbon. This is also useful for removing surface dust from ribbons that are to be gently washed.

🌿 Permanent stains are, unfortunately, permanent. Often, especially on vintage ribbon, soiling such as watermarks, blotches, and various other impermeable stains add to the already present patina of age. Better to leave well enough alone if the above methods don't produce the desired results. A great many people prefer vintage things to look just that—vintage.

PURCHASING RIBBON

Ribbon quality: It is important to purchase ribbon of the highest quality for many reasons, the most important being that the quality of the ribbon determines in large part how well any project or embellishment will turn out. Unfortunately, inexpensive ribbon looks inexpensive, and this will translate to your project or embellishment. Higher quality ribbon may

be higher priced, but it is usually more supple, a finer weave, and heirloom quality. Look for ribbons made of silk, rayon, cotton, or acetate. There are some polyester ribbons, especially taffetas, that are of good quality, but many of the novelty ribbons made of polyester are not. When shopping for ribbon, always buy more than you think you need; if you find a lovely ribbon you want to purchase without a specific project in mind, remember that a good rule of thumb is to purchase no less than four yards, which is enough for almost any project.

Ribbon sizes: Most ribbons available today come in sizes from 1/8 inch up to 5 inches, with 1-1/2 inches being the most common. Vintage ribbons can still be found that are wider, and if you come across those, don't pass them up! Technically, any woven material 18 inches wide or less can be considered ribbon.

Generally, it pays to have on hand several colors of satin, taffeta, and velvet in 1-inch widths and a few in 1-1/2-inch widths for any projects or packages. Several colors of satin in the 1/8-inch width are also good for a variety of applications. Wider taffetas and satins are perfect for more extravagant gift presentations or décor.

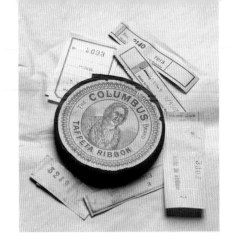

STORING RIBBON

Properly storing ribbon keeps it protected and ready to use when the need arises. No one likes to search for things or have to prepare them before they can be used, especially if you regularly have projects or events that require ribbon. Ribbon, like most textiles and paper, should never be stored in sunlight and is preferably stored in a cool, dry place. If you collect vintage and antique textiles and ribbons, it's even more important to store them correctly for preservation purposes.

Spool or roll: For nonvintage items, keep the ribbon on the spool or roll it up loosely, keeping it neat. Use a ribbon box with grommets on the side that allow you to pull out the amount you need to cut. This is an attractive method of storing ribbon in a work space or studio. These boxes can be purchased at craft supply stores or can be made by adapting a long, narrow box with a grommet kit.

Figure 8: This is a good way to store ribbon for later use when you don't have a spool or you need to gather a large amount in a neat fashion very quickly. Start by making an "L" with the index finger and thumb of your left hand. Hold the end of the ribbon between your middle finger and thumb. With your right hand, wind the ribbon back and forth over your index finger and middle finger/thumb in a figure 8 pattern. When nearly all the ribbon is looped, take the remaining "tail" and wrap it around the center of the figure 8, tucking it in. This holds it together and allows you to pull ribbon from the center as if pulling tissue from a box.

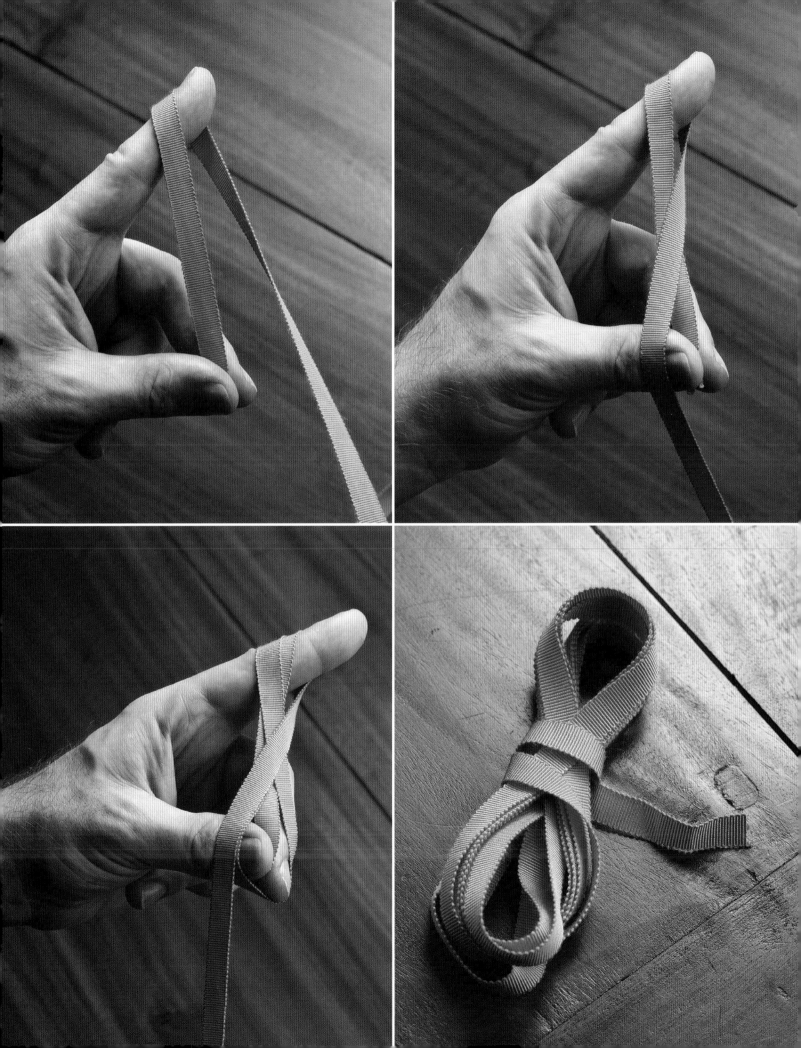

NEW YORK
MERCANTILE COMPANY
140-142 W. 5TH ST. CIN'TI. O.

NEW YORK
MERCANTILE COMPANY
140-142 W. 5TH ST. CIN'TI. O.

NEW
MER
140-142

NÔTRE - DAME PLACE VENDÔME RIV

Acid-free boxes and tissue: Essential for delicate vintage ribbons and even more so for antique pieces, acid-free products are the first step in safeguarding textiles. Items can be layered in these protective boxes between sheets of acid-free tissue away from dust and light and then stored in an appropriately cool, dry place. For extremely rare and valuable pieces, a pair of light cotton gloves of the sort used by preservationists should be worn when handling vintage swatch books, *facing, above left, and above right.*

One can create a personal swatch book for decorative or artistic use; here, each ribbon sample is held to the page by a cut-out of a Corinthian capital, an inventive way to hide raw ends, *right.*

Ribbon Glossary

antique: An item one hundred years old or older (in America). Europeans tend to consider items antique if they are two hundred years or more old.

bias-cut silk ribbon: A type of ribbon, often of silk or rayon, cut on the bias (at a 45-degree angle). A bias-cut gives ribbon stretch in two directions and, thus, great draping quality.

brocade: A ribbon woven with a raised pattern overall, usually floral or figurative in style. Brocade often has gold or silver threads woven into the design.

bullion: Ribbon trim with coiled metal threads couched onto the surface, creating beautiful three-dimensional patterns. Due to the intricacy and time it takes to produce, it is usually quite expensive. A lot of bullion is manufactured in India, where they have perfected the methods used in its creation.

chenille: Ribbon with a velvety tufted appearance, hence the name *chenille,* which is French for "caterpillar."

cockade: A rosette of ribbon worn as a decorative element or a symbol of rank.

damask: A patterned, reversible woven fabric, traditionally of silk.

double-faced: Indicates ribbon that has the exact same appearance on both sides.

embroidered: Ribbon with a hand- or machine-stitched design over the surface; the threads from the embroidery show on the reverse of the ribbon.

grosgrain: A ribbed woven ribbon, traditionally used by milliners to decorate and finish hats. Authentic French grosgrain (rayon and cotton) is woven on a shuttle loom, which creates a natural, delicate picot edge.

iridescent: Ribbon woven with two different-colored threads warp and weft, creating a lustrous, rainbow-like effect that changes colors with the angle from which it is viewed.

jacquard: Ribbon woven on a jacquard loom. The loom, invented in France by Joseph Marie Jacquard in 1804, creates a figured weave by using endless belts of pattern cards punched with holes and arranged in repeated patterns. Brocade, damask, and jacquard ribbons are made using jacquard looms.

metallic: A ribbon woven with metal threads. Originally made from actual gold and silver threads, metallic ribbons, along with bullions and brocades, were often worn only by royalty and church hierarchy.

moiré: A pattern of ribbon said to have originated in the eighteenth century when a courtier suffered a water spill on her elegant silk gown, thus giving it a "water-marked" effect. This pattern has been given many names, such as watered silk, silk moiré, or simply moiré. Today, moiré is made from passing ribbed fabric or ribbon between two cylinders so part of the ribs in the weave are flattened while others remain unflattened. The resulting contrast reflects light to give the moiré effect. Moiré is derived from the French *moirer,* "to water."

ombre: A type of ribbon consisting of a single color blending from light to dark across the width, such as pale lavender to dark purple.

organdy: Diaphanous ribbon made of very fine threads woven openly, creating an incredibly light and translucent appearance.

picot: Continuous small decorative loops forming an ornamental edging. You will find this type of edge on many vintage ribbons; it is not made as often today.

plaid: Bands of different-colored threads in various widths woven together warp and weft in the body of the ribbon produce this classic Scottish pattern.

printed ribbon: Ribbon, usually taffeta, that is first milled and then processed through a stamping or inking machine to apply a painted or foil design.

reversible: Ribbon woven so the pattern on the "front" is shown in reverse, along with its colors, on the "back."

ribbon: Narrow woven bands measuring in width from 1/16 inch up to 18 inches. Anything over 18 inches wide is considered fabric. Most ribbon comes in widths starting at 1/8 inch and going up to 1-1/2 inches. Larger sizes are sometimes hard to find but are generally available in 2-3/4 and 4 inches.

ribbon trims: Plain ribbon that is gathered, folded, or stitched to create a new design. Trims can be handmade or machine-made. A single ribbon trim can also be made of a combination of several different ribbons. Other elements such as beads, buttons, and embroidery can be used on ribbon trim.

ricrac: A trim with a zigzag design, usually of cotton or polyester, that can be found in velvet as a novelty trim. This is the popular trim from the 1970s, seen on dresses, bibs, draperies, and any number of items.

rococo: A design made up of narrow ribbons stitched together to create an intricate floral-like pattern. Rococo is often delicate in appearance and is used on young girls' finer dresses or as a decorative trim on soft goods for the home.

ruched ribbon: Plain ribbon gathered in the center or on either side to create a puckered or loosely pleated effect. From the old French *ruche,* meaning "beehive," this is also considered a ribbon trim.

satin: A particular weave that gives ribbon a luxuriously glossy surface. Satin can be single- or double-faced. It is the most widely used ribbon, and silk satin is the finest.

seam binding: A binding usually made of cotton or rayon used to finish hems on garments. It is often used for decorative purposes as well, such as packaging.

selvedge: The edge of woven fabrics, finished to prevent unraveling. Ribbon often has a decorative selvedge, like picot.

silk: Ribbon woven from the threads of the silkworm. It is usually the most expensive type of ribbon one can buy. Most fine ribbons were made of silk (and available to relatively few) until the mid-nineteenth century, when acetate and rayon were invented. These new fibers offered less expensive alternatives with similar properties and appearance.

single-faced: Ribbon, usually satin, that has a proper front, as opposed to its reverse, which usually has a noticeably dull finish.

soutache: A narrow, flat braid used for ornamental work.

striped: Among the most popular of ribbon styles. Commonly made in grosgrain or taffeta, it can also be found in silk, satin, or velvet. Stripes can be woven in or printed on the ribbon.

taffeta: A flat-woven ribbon with a matte finish. It can be made of various fibers, such as silk, rayon, or polyester. Taffeta comes in checks, plaids, solids, iridescents, stamped, variegated, or ombres. It usually has a wired edge (which can be removed) but is also available unwired.

variegated: A ribbon with two (sometimes three) different colors blending together across its width.

velvet: Ribbon with a thick plush pile or napped face to it. Velvet is available single- or double-faced. The word "velvet" comes from the Latin word *vellus,* meaning "fleece."

vintage: Ribbon that is at least fifty years old.

warp: The lengthwise threads in woven fabric.

weft: The horizontal threads from selvedge to selvedge in woven fabric.

wire-edge ribbon: Ribbon with a fine wire (usually of copper) woven inside each selvedge. This allows the ribbon to hold its shape when fashioned into bows, swags, ribbon flowers, and so on. The wire can be removed if desired. Wire-edge ribbons were first popularized by the French. The most popular ones are made of taffeta, but they can also be found in satin, metallics, and many other patterns.

Above: Various types of ribbon, from left to right, top to bottom: moiré taffeta with satin edge, rayon trim, polka dot, wired novelty ribbon, satin stripe, wired tassel trim, taffeta with decorative edge, taffeta with satin decorative edge, satin taffeta with wired edge, satin rococo, iridescent organdy, printed taffeta with wired edge, double-faced satin, organdy with ruffled edge, velvet, taffeta with satin stripe and wired edge, satin with ruffled edge, double-faced satin with picot edge, plaid taffeta with wired edge, jacquard satin, velvet ricrac, solid grosgrain, narrow taffeta with lettuce edge, satin cord (rattail), silk dupioni plaid, iridescent taffeta with wired edge, taffeta with scalloped picot edge, ombre taffeta with wired edge, and wide taffeta with satin stripes.

Resources

The following is a list of all the wonderful people and places we have used in the creation of this book. We hope these great resources will help inspire you to create wonderful things for your next project or event.

Nicholas Kniel—Fine Ribbons and Embellishments
290 Hilderbrand, B-16
Atlanta, GA 30328
404-252-8855
www.nicholaskniel.com

All of the ribbons featured in this book can be found at Nicholas Kniel. We also carry fine buttons, feathers, flowers, German glass glitter and paper Dresdens, masks, new and vintage millinery items, Swarovski crystals, and other embellishments.

Parker Smith Photography
1167B Zonolite Place
Atlanta, GA 30306
404-313-6030
www.parkersmithphoto.com

Over the years we have worked with Parker on many projects. He is the finest photographer we know, and he specializes in portrait and commercial photography. A visit to his studio is always a source of excitement and inspiration.

Addison Endpapers
6397 Telegraph
Oakland, CA 94609

The talented Julie Addison creates beautiful designs and unique paper goods using the vintage presses and ephemera in her studio.

Arrangements by Catherine
By Appointment
Atlanta, GA 30328
404-847-9843
www.arrangementsatl.com

Catherine Walthers is a brilliant floral designer whose creations never cease to amaze us, whether for intimate soirées or grand weddings. She is a delight to work with and her exacting standards ensure no event will be less than absolutely perfect.

Anne Barge
79 West Paces Ferry Road
Atlanta, GA 30305
404-873-8076
www.annebarge.com

Anne's gowns are truly exceptional, with an unrivaled attention to detail and quality. She uses the finest silks and her French laces are superb. She and her talented staff take great pleasure in creating beautiful gowns for brides, and her atelier is a warm and sumptuous place to visit.

Badgley Mischka
2800 A North Druid Hills Road
Atlanta, GA 30329
404-873-8070
www.badgleymischkabride.com

The design duo of Mark Badgley and James Mischka, known as Badgley Mischka, specializes in glamorous day wear and evening wear along with their bridal dress collection. These timelessly elegant gowns are inspired by the Hollywood glamour of the 1940s.

Jodi Battaglia
1603 Exeter Court
Marietta, GA 30068
www.jodibattaglia.com

The one-of-a-kind stuffed animals created by this artist are true works of art. Jodi crafts each from start to finish of the finest materials, adding a delightful touch of whimsy here and there.

Beadazzles
290 Hilderbrand Drive, B-15
Atlanta, GA 30328
404-843-8606

An Atlanta institution, run by the knowledgeable and discerning Alice Walker, this store is a treasure trove of beads, crystals, and findings.

Beverly Bremer Silver Shop
3164 Peachtree Road NW
Atlanta, GA 30305
404-261-4009
www.beverlybremer.com

Beverly Bremer truly is the place to go for silver in Atlanta. With her selection and expert guidance, one will always find the perfect piece.

The Biltmore Ballrooms
817 West Peachtree Street NW
Atlanta, GA 30308
404-962-8704
www.novareevents.com

Built in 1924, these spectacular as well as historic special event spaces can accommodate groups from 50 to 1,500 for a truly memorable and elegant experience.

Black Tie by Lori
6021 Sandy Springs Circle
Atlanta, GA 30328
www.brdailsbylori.com

Black Tie by Lori offers the largest selection of rental and retail formal wear in the Southeast. In addition, they have fine men's suits and custom tailored shirts.

Bobbe Gillis Gallery and Fine Framing
Brick Works at Midtown West
1000 Marietta Street NW
Suite 108
Atlanta, GA 30328
404-347-9016
www.gillisgallery.com

Bobbe Gillis and her warm, creative gallery staff are superbly attuned to the needs of clients, both individual and corporate, when it comes to choosing, framing, and installing fine works of art.

Classic Cheesecakes & Cakes
3125 Shadowlawn Avenue
Atlanta, GA 30305
404-233-9636
www.classiccheesecakes.com

Owner Mark Lotti uses the finest ingredients to create his classic and often whimsical cakes. We consider them masterpieces of design and taste!

Crane & Co.
30 South Street
Dalton, MA 01226
www.crane.com

Crane stationery products are among the finest made today, and have been for more than two hundred years. Their quality is unsurpassed.

Creative Table, Inc.
408 South Atlanta Street
Suite 140
Roswell, GA 30075
800-992-1105
www.creative-tables.com

Creative Tables, Inc., a national specialty linen rental company, offers an extensive collection of high quality table linen rentals, chair covers, napkins, skirting, and decorative trim.

Dolce
8601 Dunwoody Place
Suite 304
Atlanta, GA 30350
404-255-9530
www.dolceinc.com

Laura Weiss, owner of Dolce, specializes in custom gourmet edible favors for parties and weddings, corporate gifts, and gift baskets. We love the vast array of colors she has for M&Ms.

Ernest Gaspard & Associates
351 Peachtree Hills Avenue
Suite 109
Atlanta, GA, 30350
404-233-8645
www.ernestgaspard.com

All the finest fabrics, furniture, wall coverings and accessories any exacting client might hope for. Ernest Gaspard carries over 70 lines in his showroom at the Atlanta Decorative Arts Center.

Anna Griffin
www.annagriffin.com

For a wonderful selection of quality invitations for weddings and showers, birthdays and holidays, or any special event throughout the year, Anna Griffin is a must-go-to.

Fiskars
2537 Daniels Street
Madison, WI 53718
866-348-5661
www.fiskars.com

Fiskars makes great quality shears and rotary products for use in creating gorgeous decorative cuts to finish the ends of your ribbons. I use them regularly in many of our projects, and, of course, in the store.

Fragile
6010 Sandy Springs Circle NE, #C
Atlanta, GA 30328
404-257-1323
www.fragilegifts.com

A destination for those looking for the perfect stemware or china, Fragile is a dream for brides-to-be and anyone who wants exceptional table and tabletop giftware.

Havens
3209 Paces Ferry Place
Suite 6
Atlanta, GA 30305
404-239-0411
www.havensonline.com

If you love chic, romantic clothes with an emphasis on the feminine, look to Havens. Whenever I need clothing for a photo shoot, one of the first places I go is to Havens. They always have the perfect, out-of-the-ordinary pieces I'm looking for.

Lewis & Sheron Textile Co.
912 Huff Road
Atlanta, GA 30318
404-351-4833
www.lsfabrics.com

Lewis & Sheron Textile Co. was founded in 1944 and has been helping Atlanta decorate its homes for more than six decades. Their huge sixty-thousand-square-foot store has been family owned and operated for four generations and still serves designers and the public with their quality, selection, and expertise.

Legends Sports Gallery
1505 Main Street Village
Hilton Head Island, SC 29926
843-681-4444
www.legendssportsgallery.net

For the sports memorabilia enthusiast, Legends has an excellent selection of collectible memorabilia from vintage items to original works of art and limited-edition prints.

Jeffrey Atlanta
3500 Peachtree Road NE, #A3
Atlanta, GA 30326
404-841-0215
www.jeffreyatlanta.com

If you have a shoe fetish like I do, you will love the shoes at Jeffrey's. This high-end clothing and shoe boutique carries the best designer shoes we all crave.

The Moore Agency
165 West Wieuca Road NE
Suite 102
Atlanta, GA 30342
404-252-8415
www.themooreagency.net

The Moore Agency specializes in red carpet looks, including bridal, fashion, and special events. From career women to celebs and socialites, the creative team at The Moore Agency caters to each client with warmth and an appreciation for each individual's taste.

Paces Papers by Jackie
110 East Andrews Drive NW
Atlanta, GA 30305
404-231-1111
www.pacespapers.com

Atlanta's finest stationery store, Paces Papers offers the largest selection of European and handmade papers in the Southeast. Their custom designed wedding and party invitations reflect the sophistication, style, and unique taste of their clients.

Paper Source
888-PAPER-11
www.paper-source.com

One of our favorite resources for paper and paper goods, Paper Source has been one of the premier purveyors of extraordinary papers and distinctive paper products since 1983.

Partners Printing
1706 Defoor Place
Atlanta, GA 30318
404-352-5885
www.partnersprinting.net

Michael Goode, owner of Partners Printing since 1977, has been offering Atlanta high-quality custom printing and finishing services while specializing in social invitations, unique papers, and creative layout and design.

Oh! Fine Lingerie
178 Peachtree Hills Avenue
Atlanta, GA 30305
404-949-9901
www.ohfinelingerie.com

With their incredible selection of new and vintage lingerie and haute couture items, this charming and slightly outré boutique is sure to capture your imagination as it does ours every time we walk in the door.

Quartet Visual Communication Products
ACCO Brands Corporation
300 Tower Parkway
Lincolnshire, IL 60069
800-541-0094
www.acco.com

We have been using Quartet bulletin boards for many years. The quality is excellent, and they lend themselves perfectly to creating the fabric and ribbon-embellished French boards we make for ourselves and our clients.

Barbara Schriber Designs, Inc.
615 Baldy Mountain Road
Sandpoint, ID 83864
208-255-7741
www.barbaraschriberdesigns.com

Barbara Schriber Designs, Inc. specializes in hand-made vintage-inspired gifts showcasing real German glass glitter, quality papers, and splendid things from the Victorian and Edwardian eras.

Southern Embroidery Works
227 Sandy Springs Place
Suite 408
Sandy Springs, GA 30328
404-705-8884
www.southernembroideryworks.com

For the best in monogramming, Southern Embroidery Works more than makes the grade. There, one can have heirloom-quality embroidery applied to almost anything. The monograms for the ribbons in this book were executed by their excellent craftspeople.

Swarovski
www.swarovski.com

We use Swarovski crystals on almost everything we create, including masks, dresses, pointe shoes, and ribbons. Everyone loves a touch of sparkle, and Swarovski knows how to produce the most beautiful crystal in a wide range of colors, styles, and sizes with quality old-world craftsmanship.

Sweet Pockets, LLC
Irwin Street Market
660 Irwin Street
Atlanta, GA 30312
404-668-1022
www.sweet-pockets.com

Lennie King makes the most scrumptious cupcakes from scratch using her own exacting recipes. Each cupcake is filled with a pocket of delicious sweet filling, hence the name.

Marlean Tucker Calligrapher
Smyrna, GA
404-963-5227
www.marleantucker.com

With her unerring eye and breathtakingly gorgeous calligraphy, this truly talented artist helped to create the gorgeous invitations used in this book.

Yves Delorme
3230 Roswell Road
Atlanta, GA
404-848-9110
www.yvesdelorme.com

Exquisite French linens woven of natural fibers in the finest European tradition, the Yves Delorme collection is distinguished by the uncompromising quality and meticulous attention to detail that is the heritage of French couture. Visiting this boutique is always a treat.

We Rent Atlanta
2716 NE Expressway
Atlanta, GA 30345
404-633-2727
www.werentatlanta.com

We Rent Atlanta has high-end rental and special event equipment, including tables, chairs, stages, dance floors, china, glassware, and catering supplies. They can also custom color chairs, or custom build anything from tables to lighting design to fit your event. They are wonderful to work with and their pick-up-and-deliver service is great!

Acknowledgments

Lisa Anderson/Gibbs Smith: For giving us the opportunity to share our vision and love of ribbon with the world.

Parker Clayton Smith: For the stunning photography. You are a master of lighting and a wonderful photographer.

Catherine Walther: For being a constant source of inspiration and a joy to have had onboard for this project. The evenings spent at your workshop designing arrangements with a glass (or several) of wine were fantastic.

Kimberly Kennedy: For simply being excited with us over anything cool and artistic; for your spirited encouragement, all your advice, and the happiness in knowing we are friends with someone so talented and vibrant.

Mary Kumpf: For all the flea markets, for being such a wonderful friend, and for everything you did for us.

Steve Moore: For your generosity, and for making everyone so gorgeous.

Gailen Rosenberg: For helping us in more ways than you realize. Your personal involvement, generosity of time (and vehicle!), and constancy as a friend helped to bring this project to fruition.

Our parents and families: For being there, encouraging us, and being proud of us, and for all the years of love and guidance.

Models: Lily Kelley, Tanna Krewson, Melissa Mitchell, Elizabeth Moseley, Susan Nicholson, Elizabeth Rosenberg, Tabb Shoup.

Pet Models: Cooper (French bulldog), Charlie (pug), Cusco (French bulldog), Pat's for Joy (horse), Punicci (Italian greyhound).

Thank you to Julie Addison, Becca Adler, Khadijah Al-Hakeem, Patrick and Lorrie Allegra, Jack Allman, Donna Allman, The Atlanta Ballet, Anne Barge, David Bellevue, Marie Bensing, Wendy Bowen, Michelle Branson, Beverly Bremer, Jessica Brown, Meka Burley, J.R. and Sarah Cottingham, Brooke Exley, Suzanne Fanning, John Fitzgerald, Andrea Fritz, Bobbi Gillis, Ernest Gaspard, Amy Gorga, Anna Griffin, Carrie Hopson, Jackie Garson Howard, Christy Hubbard, Kimberly Jerguson, Robyn Joffe, Lisa Knapp, Valerie Levin, Mark Lotti, Javaun Moradi, Nelson Atkins Museum of Art, Melissa Neufeld, Lynea Perisino, Cindy Prangl, Don Purcell, Dave Reed, Michele Reidel, Sherry Ress, Teresa Richards, Scott Robinson, Sheila Rolfer, Barbara Schriber, Bobbi Sheron, Stacey Sherman, Sandy Thigpen, John Toole, Alice Walker, Laura Weiss, Scoobie West, and Kirk Whitfield.